SPIRITUAL WARFARE: ARMING THE SAINTS BOOK 1

BY PASTOR MIGUEL BUSTILLOS

I dedicate this book, first and foremost, to my Lord Jesus Christ, who has been my constant source of inspiration and guidance. Additionally, I dedicate it to my beloved wife, Michelle, whose unwavering support has sustained me through the highs and lows of ministry. Michelle, I love you dearly and I am deeply grateful for your presence in my life.

TABLE OF CONTENTS

INTRODUCTION:

Embark on a transformative journey into the realm of spiritual warfare with Pastor Miguel Bustillos, a seasoned deliverance minister with over 15 years of experience in liberating thousands of souls in the name of Jesus. In the nascent stages of his ministry, Pastor Miguel faced formidable challenges as the landscape of deliverance ministry was vastly different from what it is today. Undeterred by the lack of support and mentorship, he pursued the necessary training and education, emerging as a proficient exorcist and deliverance minister.

Drawing from his extensive knowledge and practical experience, Pastor Miguel crafted this book with a singular aim: to equip ministers and seekers with the tools and understanding needed to engage effectively in spiritual warfare. As a graduate of esteemed institutions such as the Advance Academy of Deliverance Ministry and The School of Exorcism, as well as having completed The Official Course of Exorcism in Rome, Pastor Miguel brings a wealth of expertise to this endeavor.

Through this course, participants will delve deep into the intricacies of spiritual warfare, learning how to confront and conquer the forces of darkness that seek to oppress and ensnare.

From foundational principles to advanced techniques, Pastor Miguel imparts invaluable wisdom and guidance, empowering individuals to wield the authority of Christ with confidence and efficacy.

Whether you are a seasoned minister or a curious seeker, this course offers a comprehensive roadmap to navigate the terrain of deliverance ministry. Join us on this transformative journey as we stand against the kingdom of darkness and magnify the glory of our Lord and Savior, Christ Jesus. Get ready to unlock the secrets of spiritual warfare and emerge victorious in the battle for souls.

CHAPTER 1:
Understanding Deliverance Ministry

In the realm of spiritual warfare, deliverance ministry stands as a beacon of hope, offering liberation from the shackles of demonic oppression, obsession, or possession. Rooted in biblical principles and empowered by the authority of Christ, this vital aspect of ministry is tasked with confronting the forces of darkness that seek to hinder and torment God's people.

Biblical Foundation:

The foundation of deliverance ministry finds its roots in the teachings of Scripture. In Ephesians 6:12, we are reminded that "our struggle is not against flesh and blood, but against the rulers, against the authorities, against the powers of this dark world and against the spiritual forces of evil in the heavenly realms." This passage underscores the reality of spiritual warfare and the need for believers to engage in battle against demonic forces.

Types of Demonic Influence:

1. Oppression: These manifests as physical attacks orchestrated by demonic entities. We see examples of this in the Bible, such as Job's afflictions (Job 2:7) and the demon-possessed man in the region of the Gadarenes (Mark 5:1-20).

2. Obsession: Demonic influence extends beyond the physical realm to encompass mental assaults on the mind. Instances of obsession are evident in the biblical accounts of King Saul's torment (1 Samuel 16:14-23) and the man possessed by a legion of demons (Luke 8:26-39).

3. Demonization: While born-again Christians cannot be possessed by demons due to the indwelling of the Holy Spirit (1 Corinthians 6:19), they may still experience demonic influence over their soul (mind, emotions, or will) or physical body. This form of attack highlights the ongoing spiritual battle faced by believers.

4. Demonic Possession: In rare cases, individuals may come under the full control of demonic entities, professing to be Christian yet exhibiting behaviors and manifestations indicative of possession. The biblical narrative of the boy possessed by a mute spirit illustrates this phenomenon (Mark 9:14-29).

5. Infestation: Beyond individual attacks, demons may target dwellings or objects, inflicting spiritual contamination and unrest. This type of assault underscores the pervasive nature of spiritual warfare and the need for vigilance in guarding against demonic intrusion (Matthew 12:43-45).

Conclusion:

Deliverance ministry serves as a vital component of spiritual warfare, offering hope, healing, and restoration to those ensnared by the enemy's schemes. Armed with the truth of God's Word and empowered by the authority of Christ, ministers of deliverance stand as ambassadors of freedom, leading the oppressed into the light of God's grace and salvation. As we embark on this journey of exploration and understanding, may we be equipped to confront the forces of darkness and proclaim the victory found in Christ alone.

CHAPTER 2:

The Power of Prayer in Deliverance Ministry

In the sacred arena of spiritual warfare, prayer emerges as a formidable weapon against the forces of darkness, wielding divine authority and invoking the transformative power of God's presence. In this chapter, we embark on a journey into the profound depths of prayer in deliverance ministry, exploring its various forms, biblical foundations, and ultimate efficacy in combatting spiritual oppression.

Biblical Foundation of Prayer:

The essence of prayer in deliverance ministry finds its roots in the timeless truths of Scripture, where believers are called to engage in fervent supplication and intercession on behalf of those ensnared by demonic forces. As the apostle Paul exhorts in Ephesians 6:18, "And pray in the Spirit on all occasions with all kinds of prayers and requests. With this in mind, be alert and always keep on praying for all the Lord's people."

Types of Prayers Against Demons:

1. Deliverance Prayer: This sacred form of prayer entails fervent petitions directed to God, beseeching His divine intervention and deliverance from the grip of demonic oppression or influence. In Psalm 34:17-18, we find solace in the psalmist's cry for deliverance: "The righteous cry out, and the Lord hears them; he delivers them from all their troubles. The Lord is close to the brokenhearted and saves those who are crushed in spirit."

2. Exorcism Prayers: Rooted in the unparalleled authority of Jesus Christ, exorcism prayers entail commanding demons to flee in the mighty name of Jesus. As Jesus Himself declared in Mark 16:17, "And these signs will accompany those who believe: In my name they will drive out demons; they will speak in new tongues." Similarly, in Luke 10:19, He empowered His disciples, saying, "I have given you authority to trample on snakes and scorpions and to overcome all the power of the enemy; nothing will harm you."

Sovereign Deliverance:

Amidst the fervent prayers of believers, there exists the profound reality of sovereign deliverance—wherein God, in His infinite grace and mercy, intervenes and liberates individuals from the clutches of darkness. This divine intervention transcends human effort and is a testament to the sovereign reign of God over all creation. In Psalm 34:19, we find assurance in the promise of deliverance: "The righteous person may have many troubles, but the Lord delivers him from them all."

7

Effectiveness of Prayer:

The efficacy of prayer in deliverance ministry is not merely measured by the words spoken, but by the tangible manifestations of divine intervention and liberation. Did the attacks cease? Was there a visible confrontation and subsequent expulsion of demonic forces? Did the individual experience a tangible release from the chains of bondage? These outcomes serve as poignant testimonies to the power and efficacy of prayer in the realm of spiritual warfare.

Conclusion:

As we navigate the sacred terrain of deliverance ministry, prayer emerges as a sanctified conduit through which the divine power of God is unleashed, dismantling strongholds and ushering in the transformative light of His presence. Whether through fervent deliverance prayers, authoritative exorcism prayers, or sovereign interventions orchestrated by the hand of God, prayer remains the cornerstone of victory over the forces of darkness. May we, as vessels of divine grace and agents of spiritual liberation, continue to wield the mighty weapon of prayer, advancing God's kingdom and proclaiming His victory over all the powers of darkness.

CHAPTER 3:

Understanding Demonic Entities

In the sacred tapestry of spiritual warfare, an intricate understanding of demonic entities is essential for navigating the perilous realms of deliverance ministry. In this chapter, we embark on a profound exploration of the origins, nature, and hierarchy of demons, drawing insights from ancient texts, biblical passages, and theological discourse to illuminate their malevolent influence and sinister agenda.

Origins of Demons:

Delving into ancient texts such as the Book of Enoch, we uncover the enigmatic origins of demons as the disembodied spirits of the Nephilim—a hybrid race born from the forbidden union between fallen angels and mortal women. This concept finds echoes in the biblical narrative, where Jude 1:6 alludes to the disobedience and subsequent judgment of angels, while 2 Peter 2:4 speaks of their consignment to chains of darkness.

Angel Rebellions:

The Genesis narrative unveils the tumultuous saga of angelic rebellions that reverberated throughout the celestial realms, precipitating the emergence of demonic entities. Satan's initial revolt, accompanied by a third of the angelic host, marked the genesis of spiritual conflict and cosmic warfare (Revelation 12:4). Subsequent transgressions culminated in fallen angels descending to earth and cohabiting with mortal women, giving rise to the abominable progeny known as the Nephilim (Genesis 6:1-4).

Hierarchy of Demons:

Within the infernal hierarchy, demons are arrayed in a sinister order, each bearing distinct attributes and wielding varying degrees of malevolence. From high-ranking entities like Jezebel and Leviathan to lesser spirits of torment and temptation, each demon operates within its appointed sphere of influence, ensnaring souls and perpetuating darkness (Matthew 17:21; Matthew 12:43-45; Mark 3:27).

Satanic Deception:

Central to the demonic agenda is the propagation of deception — a nefarious ploy to subvert truth, distort reality, and ensnare humanity in the web of deceit. Satan, the arch-deceiver, masquerades as an angel of light, enticing the unsuspecting with promises of power, pleasure, and prestige (2 Corinthians 11:14). Yet, the Word of God stands as an immutable bulwark against his machinations, illuminating the path of righteousness and exposing the schemes of the enemy (Ephesians 6:11).

Victory in Christ:

Amidst the swirling maelstrom of spiritual conflict, believers find solace and strength in the triumphant power of Christ. Through His sacrificial death and glorious resurrection, Jesus disarmed the powers and principalities, triumphing over them openly (Colossians 2:15). Thus, armed with the armor of God and fortified by the indwelling presence of the Holy Spirit, believers stand firm in the assurance of victory, wielding the sword of the Spirit and proclaiming the triumph of light over darkness (Ephesians 6:12; 1 John 4:4).

Conclusion:

As we traverse the shadowed corridors of deliverance ministry, let us heed the clarion call to discernment and vigilance. May we be steadfast in our faith, unyielding in our resolve, and unwavering in our allegiance to the King of kings and Lord of lords. For in Him alone do we find refuge, redemption, and resounding victory over the forces of darkness.

CHAPTER 4:

Angelic Hierarchies and Guardian Angels

In the celestial tapestry of divine creation, angels occupy a myriad of roles and ranks, each bearing unique responsibilities ordained by the hand of the Almighty. As we delve deeper into the realms of angelic hierarchies, we uncover profound truths about their nature, function, and pivotal role in the cosmic drama of spiritual warfare.

Understanding Angelic Ranks:

Within the celestial hierarchy, angels are arrayed in various ranks and orders, each delineating their sphere of influence and authority. At the pinnacle of this hierarchy stands the archangels, exemplified by Michael, Gabriel, and Raphael, who wield unparalleled power and serve as commanders of heavenly hosts (Jude 1:9; Daniel 10:13). These celestial warriors stand ready to engage in fierce battles against the forces of darkness, defending the righteous and executing divine justice.

Angelic Counsel and Divine Decrees:

Scripture unveils the existence of angelic counsel, where celestial beings congregate in the presence of God to participate in heavenly deliberations and divine decrees. As depicted in Psalm 82, these angelic assemblies serve as conduits of divine wisdom and agents of divine will, advising the Almighty on matters of cosmic significance (Psalm 82:1; Isaiah 6:2-3). Deuteronomy 32:8-9 provides further insight into this celestial counsel, highlighting God's sovereign orchestration of angelic realms for the fulfillment of His divine purposes and the advancement of His kingdom agenda.

Guardian Angels and Divine Protection:

Amidst the chaos of earthly existence, believers find solace and security in the unwavering presence of guardian angels — ministering spirits sent forth to serve the heirs of salvation (Hebrews 1:14). These celestial sentinels stand as vigilant guardians, watching over God's children with unwavering devotion and unfailing vigilance (Psalm 91:11). Whether shielding them from physical harm, guiding them through perilous paths, or ministering to their spiritual needs, guardian angels embody the divine promise of protection and providence.

Assistance in Spiritual Warfare:

In the tumultuous arena of spiritual warfare, believers are not left defenseless against the onslaught of demonic forces. Guardian angels stand ready to intervene on behalf of God's children, wielding divine authority and executing judgment upon the enemies of righteousness (Psalm 34:7). Moreover, warrior angels—mighty champions of heavenly realms—engage in fierce battles against principalities and powers, enforcing divine decrees and routing the forces of darkness (Ephesians 6:12; Revelation 12:7).

Conclusion:

As we traverse the ethereal realms of angelic hierarchies and divine guardianship, let us embrace the reality of angelic presence and invoke their aid in times of need. For in the unseen realms, celestial warriors stand as sentinels of divine grace and power, ever watchful and ever vigilant in their mission to defend and deliver God's beloved children. May we, as heirs of salvation, take refuge in the assurance of angelic protection and divine providence, trusting in God's unfailing love and sovereign care.

CHAPTER 5:

Preparation for Deliverance Ministry

In the sacred calling of deliverance ministry, preparation is paramount for effective service in the kingdom of God. As we embark on this transformative journey, let us glean wisdom from Scripture and discern the foundational principles essential for equipping and empowering deliverance ministers.

Integrity and Character:

Scripture admonishes us to uphold integrity and moral uprightness in all aspects of ministry (1 Timothy 3:1-7). A deliverance minister must shun habitual sin and pride, walking in humility and sincerity before God and man (Proverbs 11:3; James 4:6). Trustworthiness is paramount, and any deviation from ethical conduct should result in immediate removal from ministry (Proverbs 10:9; Titus 1:7-8).

Dedication to Prayer and Fasting:

The efficacy of deliverance ministry hinges upon fervent prayer and fasting, aligning our hearts with the will of God and invoking

His divine intervention (Matthew 17:21; Ephesians 6:18). A disciplined prayer life and regular fasting regimen cultivate spiritual sensitivity and fortitude, empowering ministers to engage in spiritual warfare with unwavering faith and divine authority (Mark 9:29; Acts 13:2-3).

Grounded in Scripture:

The Word of God serves as our anchor and guide in the tumultuous seas of spiritual warfare (2 Timothy 3:16-17). A deliverance minister must be a diligent student of Scripture, immersing themselves in the timeless truths of God's Word and discerning the spirits through the lens of biblical revelation (Hebrews 4:12; 1 Thessalonians 5:21). Grounded in scriptural wisdom, ministers are equipped to discern truth from deception and navigate the complexities of deliverance ministry with discernment and wisdom.

Compassion and Humility:

Central to effective deliverance ministry is a heart of compassion and humility, mirroring the love and grace of our Lord Jesus Christ (Colossians 3:12; Philippians 2:3-4). Ministers should exude sincerity, respectability, and integrity, eschewing dishonest gain and pursuing the welfare of those in spiritual bondage (Romans 12:10; Titus 2:7-8). Grounded in humility, ministers are receptive to correction and accountability, recognizing their dependence on God and His appointed overseers (Proverbs 15:22; Hebrews 13:17).

Centrality of Christ:

Above all else, deliverance ministry must be Christ-centered and gospel-focused (Colossians 1:18; 1 Corinthians 2:2). Ministers should exalt the name of Jesus and direct all glory and honor to Him, acknowledging His sovereignty and lordship over every spiritual realm (Philippians 2:9-11; Revelation 5:12). The proclamation of the gospel should remain paramount, leading souls to salvation and freedom in Christ (Mark 16:15; Acts 4:12).

Accountability and Mentorship:

No minister is an island unto themselves, but all are called to accountability and mentorship in the body of Christ (Proverbs 27:17; Galatians 6:1). Deliverance ministers should seek guidance and oversight from seasoned leaders and mentors, ensuring alignment with the vision of the ministry and safeguarding against spiritual pitfalls (1 Corinthians 4:15; Titus 2:3-5). In humble submission to authority, ministers are strengthened, corrected, and empowered for greater effectiveness in the kingdom.

Conclusion:

As we embark on the sacred vocation of deliverance ministry, let us heed the call to preparation and consecration. May integrity, prayer, scriptural grounding, compassion, humility, Christ-centeredness, and accountability serve as the bedrock of our ministry endeavors, empowering us to advance the kingdom of God and set the captives free in the mighty name of Jesus.

CHAPTER 6:

Cautionary Counsel for Deliverance Ministers

Entering the realm of deliverance ministry is akin to stepping onto the battlefield of spiritual warfare, where unseen forces of darkness wage relentless attacks against the kingdom of God. In this chapter, we delve into the sobering realities and essential precautions that deliverance ministers must embrace as they navigate the perilous path of spiritual warfare.

Perils of Spiritual Warfare:

Deliverance ministry exposes ministers to intense spiritual battles, where the enemy seeks to undermine, obstruct, and destroy the work of God. Satan, the adversary, prowls like a roaring lion, relentlessly seeking to devour and destroy those who stand in opposition to his kingdom (1 Peter 5:8). He employs subtle tactics and deceptive schemes, using individuals close to you to launch assaults on your character, faith, and ministry. Do not underestimate the adversary's cunning and persistence but stand firm in the promises of God and the authority of Christ (Ephesians 6:12).

Steadfast Faith and Vigilance:

In the face of relentless opposition and spiritual assaults, remain steadfast in your faith and resolute in your commitment to God's calling upon your life. Take refuge in the assurance of God's protection and provision, trusting in His unfailing promises to shield and deliver His faithful servants from the schemes of the evil one (Psalm 91:4-5; 2 Thessalonians 3:3). Clothed in the full armor of God, you are empowered to stand firm against the devil's schemes and emerge victorious in spiritual battles (Ephesians 6:10-18).

Wisdom and Discernment in Ministry:

Exercise discernment and wisdom in your ministry endeavors, recognizing the inherent risks and potential dangers of engaging in deliverance sessions. Never embark on deliverance alone, but always seek the companionship and support of fellow believers who can provide accountability, prayer, and assistance (Ecclesiastes 4:9-10; Proverbs 11:14). If circumstances necessitate solo ministry, consider recording the session for documentation and protection, ensuring transparency and accountability in all your dealings (Proverbs 15:22).

Maintaining Holiness and Integrity:

In all your interactions and ministry engagements, uphold the highest standards of holiness, integrity, and accountability. Exercise caution and prudence, especially when ministering to individuals of the opposite sex, by ensuring the presence of a same-gender witness or assistant to avoid any appearance of impropriety or misunderstanding (1 Thessalonians 5:22; Proverbs 4:23). Guard your heart and mind against the subtle snares of the enemy, remaining vigilant and steadfast in your devotion to God and His righteousness (Philippians 4:7; James 4:7).

Conclusion:

As you embark on the noble and challenging journey of deliverance ministry, let wisdom, discernment, and faith guide your every step. Take refuge in the shelter of the Most High, knowing that He who is in you is greater than He who is in the world (1 John 4:4). With unwavering trust in God's providence and protection, you can navigate the perilous waters of spiritual warfare with courage, confidence, and divine assurance, emerging victorious in the power and authority of Jesus Christ.

CHAPTER 7:

Preparing Individuals for Deliverance Ministry

In the sacred work of deliverance ministry, thorough preparation and discernment are essential for facilitating lasting freedom and spiritual restoration in individuals seeking deliverance. In this chapter, we explore the critical steps and biblical principles involved in preparing individuals for deliverance ministry, ensuring a foundation of faith, transparency, and spiritual readiness.

Thorough Assessment and Discernment:

Before engaging in deliverance ministry, it is imperative to conduct a comprehensive assessment of the individual's spiritual condition and history. Utilize questionnaires and interviews to gather relevant information about past activities, experiences, and potential doorways to demonic oppression (James 4:7). This discernment process provides valuable insight into the root causes of spiritual bondage and enables targeted prayer and intervention.

Seeking Guidance from the Holy Spirit:

Central to effective deliverance ministry is reliance on the leading and guidance of the Holy Spirit. As ministers, we must cultivate sensitivity to the voice of God, seeking His wisdom and direction in every aspect of ministry (John 16:13). One word from God can unlock the chains of bondage and usher in profound liberation and healing (Isaiah 30:21). Therefore, prioritize prayerful discernment and reliance on divine revelation in the ministry process.

Requirement of Transparency and Humility:

Effective deliverance hinges upon the willingness of individuals to be transparent and humble before God and His appointed ministers. Those seeking deliverance must be willing to disclose their struggles, sins, and vulnerabilities without reservation or concealment (James 5:16). Refusal to embrace transparency and humility hinders the efficacy of deliverance ministry, as pride erects barriers to the work of the Holy Spirit (1 Peter 5:5).

Assessment of Faith and Discipleship:

Assess the individual's faith and readiness to receive deliverance, discerning their level of belief and trust in God's power to set them free (Mark 9:23). If a person lacks faith or understanding in the principles of deliverance, invest time in discipling and nurturing their spiritual growth before proceeding with ministry (Romans 10:17). Discipleship and spiritual mentoring are essential components of the deliverance process, equipping individuals with the knowledge and faith necessary for enduring freedom (2 Timothy 2:2).

Establishment of Spiritual Support and Accountability:

Ensure that individuals seeking deliverance are connected to a supportive spiritual community and accountable relationships. Encourage active participation in church fellowship, Bible studies, and prayer groups to foster spiritual growth and accountability (Hebrews 10:24-25). Emphasize the importance of maintaining spiritual disciplines and guarding against behaviors or influences that could potentially open doors to demonic oppression (1 Corinthians 15:33; Ephesians 4:27).

Conclusion:

As ministers of deliverance, our role is to facilitate the journey of individuals towards spiritual freedom and wholeness in Christ. By adhering to biblical principles of assessment, discernment, transparency, humility, and discipleship, we lay a solid foundation for the transformative work of deliverance ministry. May we continue to rely on the guidance of the Holy Spirit and the power of God's Word, leading individuals into the abundant life and liberty found in Jesus Christ alone (John 8:36).

CHAPTER 8:

Unveiling Deliverance Terminology

In the realm of deliverance ministry, understanding key terminology is crucial for effective spiritual warfare and liberation from demonic oppression. In this chapter, we delve into essential deliverance terminology, illuminating their significance and biblical foundations.

Demonic Legal Right:

Demonic legal rights denote the authorization or permission granted to demons to exert influence or control over an individual's life. This legal foothold is often established through sin or ungodly activities, providing demons with a basis for their presence and operation (Genesis 4:7). By addressing and renouncing these legal rights through repentance and spiritual warfare, individuals can revoke the authority of demonic forces and experience deliverance from their influence.

Stronghold:

A stronghold refers to a fortified belief system or mindset established by the enemy in a person's life (2 Corinthians 10:3-4).

These strongholds are rooted in deception and falsehood, shaping perceptions and behaviors contrary to God's truth. Through repetitive exposure to lies and deception, demons entrench themselves behind these strongholds, hindering individuals from embracing the liberating truth of God's Word. Deliverance from strongholds necessitates the dismantling of false beliefs through the transformative power of God's truth.

Infestation:

Infestation denotes the infiltration and occupation of a dwelling or object by demonic entities. This phenomenon extends beyond individual possession to encompass environments or physical spaces influenced or controlled by demonic forces. Deliverance from infestation involves spiritual cleansing and the expulsion of demonic presence from the affected area, restoring it to alignment with God's purposes and protection.

Possession:

While born-again Christians cannot be demon possessed, they can experience varying degrees of demonic influence or oppression (1 John 4:4). Possession entails the complete control and domination of an individual's faculties by demonic entities, resulting in the suppression of their will and identity. Deliverance from demonic possession requires spiritual intervention and the assertion of God's authority over the invading forces, restoring the individual to freedom and wholeness in Christ.

Demonic Imprint:

Demonic imprinting occurs when individuals perceive lingering effects of demonic influence despite undergoing deliverance. This deceptive tactic employed by the enemy seeks to instill fear, doubt, and uncertainty in the individual's mind, perpetuating a false sense of demonic presence. By anchoring their faith in the finished work of Christ and resisting the lies of the enemy, individuals can dispel these deceptive imprints and walk in the fullness of their deliverance (James 4:7).

Conclusion:

As we unravel the intricacies of deliverance terminology, may we glean wisdom and discernment to engage effectively in spiritual warfare. By aligning ourselves with the truth of God's Word and exercising the authority bestowed upon us as believers, we can confront and overcome the strategies of the enemy, experiencing the transformative power of deliverance and restoration in Christ. Let us stand firm in the assurance of God's victory and liberation, knowing that through Him, we are more than conquerors over every spiritual stronghold and oppression (Romans 8:37).

CHAPTER 9:

Addressing Demonic Infestations in Dwellings and Objects

In the realm of spiritual warfare, it is essential to recognize and confront demonic infestations that may manifest within dwellings or attach themselves to objects. While the Bible does not explicitly mention demons dwelling in objects, instances such as the possession of pigs in Matthew 8:28-34 suggest their ability to inhabit physical entities. Therefore, it is imperative to understand how to address and eradicate demonic influence in dwellings and objects according to biblical principles.

Identifying Cursed Objects:

The first step in addressing demonic infestations is to identify cursed objects within the dwelling. This may involve discernment through prayer or seeking guidance from individuals with spiritual insight. Once identified, these cursed objects must be dealt with decisively to prevent further spiritual contamination (Acts 19:19).

Proper Disposal and Prayer of Deliverance:

Cursed objects should be subjected to prayers of deliverance, similar to those employed in the liberation of demonized individuals. Utilize prayers of Psalm 109 as a spiritual weapon against the forces of darkness, invoking the power and authority of Jesus Christ to break the curse and release God's protection and blessing (Psalm 109:26-31). Following prayer, the cursed objects must be destroyed and disposed of properly to prevent them from falling into the hands of others and perpetuating spiritual harm.

Home Exorcism and Spiritual Cleansing:

In cases of demonic infestation within dwellings, a home exorcism may be necessary to cleanse the premises of demonic presence and influence. Engage in fervent prayer, commanding all demonic entities to leave the house in the name of Jesus Christ (Luke 10:19). Declare the authority of Jesus Christ over the property, evicting all trespassing demons and reclaiming the dwelling as a sanctuary for God's presence (Matthew 18:18). Anoint every door and room with blessed oil as a symbolic representation of the Holy Spirit's presence, sealing the premises with divine protection and sanctification (James 5:14).

Conclusion:

By adhering to biblical principles of spiritual warfare and deliverance, we can effectively confront and eradicate demonic infestations in dwellings and objects. Through prayer, discernment, and unwavering faith in the authority of Jesus Christ, we can secure God's protection and blessing over our homes and possessions, ensuring that they serve as sanctuaries of His presence and glory. Let us stand firm in our identity as children of God, equipped with the power and authority to overcome every scheme of the enemy and walk in freedom and victory (1 John 4:4; Ephesians 6:12).

Certainly, here are prayers for addressing demonic infestations and conducting spiritual cleansing:

Prayer for Deliverance from Cursed Objects:

"Dear Heavenly Father,

I come before You in the name of Jesus Christ, recognizing Your sovereignty and authority over all things, including the spiritual realm. I acknowledge that cursed objects have no power or authority over me, for I am covered by the blood of Jesus and sealed by the Holy Spirit.

In the mighty name of Jesus, I renounce and break any curse associated with these objects. I declare that they have no place in my life or my dwelling. I command every demonic influence attached to these objects to be bound and cast out, never to return.

I cover myself, my family, and my home with the protective blood of Jesus, and I declare that no weapon formed against us shall prosper. I thank You, Lord, for Your deliverance and cleansing power. May Your peace and presence dwell in our midst, guarding us against all spiritual attacks.

In Jesus' name, I pray. Amen."

Prayer for Home Exorcism and Spiritual Cleansing:

"Heavenly Father,

I come before You in the name of Jesus Christ, acknowledging Your authority over all creation. I stand firm in the power of Your Word and the victory won for us through the cross.

I declare that this home belongs to Jesus Christ and serves as a sanctuary for Your presence. I command every demonic entity trespassing on this property to leave immediately, in the name of Jesus. I break every stronghold and curse over this dwelling, releasing Your freedom and blessing.

I anoint every door and room with blessed oil, symbolizing the presence of the Holy Spirit. May Your divine protection and peace reign within these walls, guarding us against all spiritual attacks and influences.

I thank You, Lord, for Your faithfulness and protection. Let Your light shine brightly in this home, dispelling all darkness and establishing Your kingdom's rule.

In Jesus' name, I pray. Amen."

These prayers can be personalized and adapted according to specific circumstances and spiritual needs. It's important to pray with faith and conviction, trusting in God's power to bring deliverance and restoration.

CHAPTER 10:

Understanding Demonization and Possession

In the realm of spiritual warfare, discerning between demonization and possession is crucial for effective deliverance ministry. Let's delve deeper into these concepts, their manifestations, and the biblical principles guiding accurate diagnosis and intervention.

Defining Demonization:

Demonization encompasses the partial or temporary control exerted by demonic forces over an individual's mind, body, or spirit. It can manifest in various forms, including oppressive thoughts, compulsive behaviors, or physical ailments.

Exploring Possession and Diagnosis:

Possession occurs when an evil spirit gains complete control over an individual, often leading to trance-like states or loss of consciousness. Discerning possession requires careful observation and spiritual insight.

Distinguishing Oppression and Mental Illness:

While external oppression may result in physical manifestations such as bruises or scratches, internal oppression affects the individual's mental and emotional well-being. Differentiating these from mental illness is crucial for accurate diagnosis and treatment.

Biblical Insight:

Scriptures such as Ephesians 6:12 remind us that our struggle is not against flesh and blood but against spiritual forces of evil. Understanding this spiritual reality is essential for effective spiritual warfare.

Identifying Demonization:

Various biblical accounts, including those of Jesus casting out demons (Matthew 8:16) and Paul's encounters with possessed individuals (Acts 16:16-18), provide insights into the manifestations of demonization.

Signs of Demonization:

1. Unexplained Diseases or Conditions: Individuals may exhibit ailments that defy medical explanation, indicating spiritual influence.
2. Ineffective Medications: Despite medical treatment, symptoms persist, suggesting a deeper spiritual root.
3. Resistance to Prayer or Religious Items: Aversion to prayer or religious symbols like the cross may indicate demonic activity.

4. Physical Marks: Unexplained scratches or bruises may appear on the individual's body, often without apparent cause.

5. Supernatural Manifestations: Speaking in strange tongues, displaying extraordinary strength, or possessing knowledge beyond natural means.

6. Involvement in Sin or the Occult: Individuals with a history of habitual sin or occult involvement may be more susceptible to demonization.

7. Ancestral Influence: Generational ties to occult practices, satanism, or Freemasonry can open doors to demonic oppression.

8. Resistance to Treatment: Lack of response to conventional medications or therapies may suggest a spiritual component to the ailment.

9. Auditory Hallucinations: Voices heard in the mind, especially those contradicting biblical truths, may indicate demonic influence.

10. Mental Confusion or Scattered Thoughts: Inability to focus or persistent mental fog, particularly during spiritual encounters, may signal spiritual warfare.

11. Interference with Prayer: Individuals may struggle to pray or experience difficulty in hearing or repeating prayers, indicating spiritual hindrance.

By recognizing these signs and relying on biblical principles and the guidance of the Holy Spirit, deliverance ministers can effectively combat demonic influence and bring freedom to those in need.

Not every individual will display all the signs of demonization or possession. Therefore, it is paramount for deliverance ministers to conduct thorough assessments and inquire wisely into the spiritual and personal history of those seeking deliverance. The application and interview process serves as a critical step in understanding the individual's experiences, struggles, and potential spiritual influences.

Through strategic questioning and discernment guided by the Holy Spirit, ministers can uncover hidden spiritual strongholds, past involvement in occult practices, familial influences, and other factors contributing to the individual's condition. This investigative phase allows ministers to gather essential information, identify patterns, and discern the root causes of spiritual oppression or affliction.

Furthermore, the application and interview process provide an opportunity for ministers to establish trust and rapport with the individual seeking deliverance. By fostering a safe and supportive environment, ministers can encourage openness, honesty, and transparency, facilitating a deeper understanding of the person's spiritual journey and current challenges.

Ultimately, the diligence and discernment exercised during the application and interview phase equip deliverance ministers to tailor their approach, prayers, and interventions according to the specific needs and circumstances of each individual. This personalized approach maximizes the effectiveness of deliverance ministry and enhances the likelihood of spiritual breakthrough and transformation in the lives of those seeking freedom from demonic influence.

CHAPTER 11:
Seeking Medical Assistance

Knowing When to Consult for a Medical Evaluation or Psychologist:

1. Suicidal Tendencies: If someone expresses suicidal thoughts or behaviors, it is crucial to seek immediate medical help. Proverbs 18:14 reminds us, "The spirit of a man will sustain his infirmity, but a wounded spirit who can bear?" We must recognize the seriousness of mental distress and seek professional assistance.

2. Self-Harm: Individuals engaging in self-harming behaviors should be evaluated by medical professionals. In 1 Corinthians 6:19-20, we are reminded that our bodies are temples of the Holy Spirit, and we are called to honor God with our bodies. Seeking medical help is an act of honoring the sanctity of life.

3. History of Mental Illness: Those with a known history of mental health issues should receive ongoing medical care. Psalm 34:17-18 assures us that the Lord is near to the

brokenhearted and saves the crushed in spirit. Seeking medical support is part of God's provision for healing and restoration.

4. Combative Behavior: Individuals exhibiting combative behaviors, such as refusal to eat or drink, may require medical intervention. James 5:14-15 encourages us to call the elders of the church to pray over the sick and anoint them with oil in the name of the Lord. This process can include seeking medical professionals for physical care.

5. Lack of Improvement: If a person's condition does not improve with prayer or spiritual interventions, medical evaluation may be necessary. Proverbs 15:22 advises us that plans fail for lack of counsel, but with many advisers, they succeed. Seeking medical advice is wise and aligns with biblical principles of seeking wisdom.

Working with the Medical Community:

Collaborating with medical professionals is essential for ensuring the safety and well-being of both the minister and the individual seeking help. Establishing a team of medical experts can provide comprehensive support and guidance.

Members of the Medical Team:

1. Medical Doctor: Primary care physicians or specialists can address any underlying medical issues that require attention. Luke, the beloved physician (Colossians 4:14), exemplifies the importance of medical care in conjunction with spiritual ministry.

2. Psychiatrist: Psychiatrists can conduct evaluations and prescribe medications for mental health conditions. Psalm 147:3 reminds us that God heals the brokenhearted and binds up their wounds. Medical professionals play a role in God's healing process.

3. Psychologist: Psychologists offer evaluations and therapeutic interventions for various mental health concerns. Proverbs 20:5 tells us that the purpose in a man's heart is like deep water, but a man of understanding will draw it out. Psychologists help individuals navigate the depths of their emotions and thoughts.

4. Nurse: Nurses play a vital role in administering medications and monitoring patient care. In Luke 10:34, the Good Samaritan attends to the wounded man's needs, demonstrating the importance of compassionate care.

Avoiding Assumptions and Heroism:

It is essential for deliverance ministers to refrain from assuming that every ailment or condition is demonic in nature. While spiritual warfare is a reality, not all sicknesses or diseases have spiritual origins. When in doubt, it is better to seek medical help than to risk overlooking a genuine medical issue.

Continuing Education and Caution:

Deliverance ministers are encouraged to pursue education in mental health through reputable organizations like the American Association of Christian Counselors and the International Society of Deliverance Ministers. Understanding the distinction between spiritual and mental health issues is crucial to providing appropriate care. Remember, it is possible for both spiritual and medical factors to contribute to a person's condition. In such cases, addressing medical concerns first may be necessary before addressing spiritual matters.

CHAPTER 12:

Consequences of Sin and Legal Rights

Sin is the violation of God's law, representing a departure from His character and will (1 John 3:4). While some may deny their sinfulness, Scripture emphasizes the importance of acknowledging and confessing sin, as God promises forgiveness and cleansing to those who do (1 John 1:8-10). Additionally, failing to do what is right also constitutes sin (James 4:17). The consequences of sin are severe, leading to spiritual death (Romans 6:23) and providing a foothold for Satan's attacks (Genesis 4:7).

Legal Rights: Satan's Claim

Satan seeks legal rights over individuals to accuse and oppress them. In Luke 22:31, Jesus warns Peter that Satan desires to sift him as wheat, highlighting Satan's relentless pursuit to claim legal rights against believers. Revelation 12:10 describes Satan as the accuser of the brethren, continually seeking grounds to accuse and condemn God's people before Him.

Consequences of Sin:

1. Separation from God: Sin disrupts our relationship with God, leading to spiritual separation and estrangement from His presence (Isaiah 59:2).

2. Death: The ultimate consequence of sin is death, not only physical death but also spiritual death, resulting in eternal separation from God (Romans 6:23).

3. Bondage and Oppression: Sin enslaves and entangles us, subjecting us to bondage and oppression by demonic forces (John 8:34; 2 Peter 2:19).

4. Brokenness and Consequences: Sin brings about brokenness in our lives and the lives of others, often leading to painful consequences and suffering (Galatians 6:7-8).

5. Hindered Prayer: Unconfessed sin can hinder our prayers and block communication with God, impeding our spiritual growth and effectiveness (Psalm 66:18).

Preventing Legal Rights:

1. Repentance and Confession: Confessing and repenting of sin removes legal rights from Satan, restoring fellowship with God and strengthening our spiritual defenses (1 John 1:9; James 5:16).

2. Walking in Obedience: By living in obedience to God's Word and following His commandments, we prevent Satan from gaining legal grounds in our lives (1 Peter 5:8-9).

3. Spiritual Warfare: Engaging in spiritual warfare through prayer, fasting, and the Word of God enables us to resist Satan's schemes and overcome his attempts to claim legal rights (Ephesians 6:10-18).

4. Submission to God: Submitting ourselves fully to God and resisting the devil empowers us to stand firm and secure in our identity as children of God (James 4:7).

Conclusion:

Understanding the consequences of sin and Satan's pursuit of legal rights underscores the importance of vigilance and spiritual discernment in our walk with God. By remaining steadfast in obedience, repentance, and spiritual warfare, we can thwart Satan's efforts and experience the abundant life promised to us in Christ.

CHAPTER 13:

Understanding Curses
in Light of Scripture

Curses have been a topic of debate and discussion among believers, with differing perspectives on their significance in the life of a Christian. Two primary schools of thought exist regarding curses, each offering distinct insights into their nature and impact.

1. Curses and the Cross:

According to the first school of thought, curses lost their power over believers through the redemptive work of Jesus Christ on the cross. Galatians 3:13 declares, "But Christ has rescued us from the curse pronounced by the law. When he was hung on the cross, he took upon himself the curse for our wrongdoing" (NLT). This perspective emphasizes the efficacy of Christ's sacrifice in nullifying the effects of curses.

However, it's important to recognize that before experiencing salvation, individuals may have been subject to curses inherited from their ancestors. While salvation breaks the power of these curses, demons associated with them may still need to be expelled through deliverance (Mark 16:17).

2. The Power of Belief:

Proverbs 23:7 reveals the significance of belief in shaping one's reality: "For as he thinks in his heart, so is he." This perspective acknowledges that even after receiving salvation, individuals may still experience the effects of curses if they harbor unbelief. Such unbelief provides legal grounds for demonic activity, allowing curses to exert influence over their lives.

Examples of curses, such as the "evil eye," demonstrate the power of belief in reinforcing their effects. The "evil eye" curse, fueled by envy and malevolence, operates through the victim's belief in its potency. Similarly, word curses spoken over individuals can manifest in their lives if they accept and internalize them.

Identifying Curses:

Curses often manifest in patterns within families, affecting various aspects of life such as health, relationships, finances, and behavior. Recognizing these patterns can provide insight into the presence of curses and their impact on individuals and generations.

A Contested Perspective:

It's worth noting that some Christians maintain a belief in the continued activity of curses, even among believers. They argue that curses can still be active in the lives of Christians if they are not properly addressed through spiritual warfare and deliverance. This perspective underscores the ongoing need for vigilance and prayer in combating spiritual attacks.

Conclusion:

Understanding curses requires discernment and a balanced approach rooted in Scripture. While Christ's sacrifice has liberated believers from the power of curses, the role of belief and spiritual warfare cannot be overlooked. By aligning our beliefs with God's truth and engaging in spiritual warfare, we can overcome the influence of curses and experience the abundant life Christ offers.

Here's an example of a prayer to break curses:

"Heavenly Father, I come before you in the name of Jesus Christ, recognizing the power of curses that may be affecting my life. I acknowledge any sins, transgressions, or generational patterns in my family line that have opened the door to these curses, and I repent of them now.

In the authority of Jesus Christ, I renounce and break every curse spoken against me, whether knowingly or unknowingly, by others or by myself. I declare that I am redeemed by the blood of Jesus, and I have been set free from the power of every curse.

I specifically break the curse of [name any specific curse or area of your life where you believe curses may be active, such as health, finances, relationships, etc.]. I cancel its effects over my life and declare it null and void in Jesus' name.

I command every demon associated with these curses to leave my life now, in the name of Jesus. I close every door that has allowed them access to me, and I seal those doors with the blood of Jesus.

Lord, I ask you to release your healing, restoration, and blessings upon me as I walk in obedience to your Word. Fill me with your Holy Spirit and empower me to live a life of victory over every curse and demonic influence.

Thank you, Father, for your love, mercy, and faithfulness. I trust in your power to break every curse and bring freedom and wholeness to my life. In Jesus' name, I pray. Amen."

CHAPTER 14:

Understanding Our Tripartite Nature

In exploring the intricacies of our spiritual makeup, it's essential to delve into the biblical foundation that underpins the concept of humanity's tripartite nature and its implications for our spiritual journey.

1. Spirit, Soul, and Body:

The apostle Paul's prayer in 1 Thessalonians 5:23 encapsulates the tripartite nature of humanity: "Now may the God of peace himself sanctify you completely, and may your whole spirit and soul and body be kept blameless at the coming of our Lord Jesus Christ." This verse highlights the distinct components of our being—the spirit, which relates to our connection with God; the soul, encompassing our mind, will, and emotions; and the body, our physical vessel.

2. Redemption of the Spirit:

At the moment of salvation, our spirit undergoes a profound transformation, becoming united with the Holy Spirit (Romans 8:9) and sealed for the day of redemption (Ephesians 1:13-14).

This spiritual rebirth marks the beginning of our journey toward holiness and communion with God.

3. Renewal of the Soul:

The process of sanctification involves the continual renewal of our soul — our mind, will, and emotions — according to the truth of God's Word (Romans 12:2). Through the work of the Holy Spirit, believers are empowered to align their thoughts and desires with God's will, gradually conforming to the image of Christ (2 Corinthians 3:18).

4. Redemption of the Body:

While our spirits are immediately regenerated upon salvation, our bodies await future redemption at the return of Christ (1 Corinthians 15:51-53). The apostle Paul describes this future transformation, where our perishable bodies will be clothed with imperishable, and our mortal bodies with immortality.

5. Demonization versus Possession:

Scripture distinguishes between demonization, where demonic forces exert influence over a believer's soul and body, and demon possession, which entails total control by demonic entities. While believers cannot be possessed due to the indwelling presence of the Holy Spirit (1 Corinthians 6:19), they may still experience spiritual oppression and attack. The attacks occur in the parts being redeemed (soul) and the parts to be redeemed in the future (body).

6. Curses and Generational Influences:

The effects of curses and generational influences are often observed in patterns of dysfunction, illness, and adversity within families. These curses may stem from ancestral sin or involvement in occult practices (Exodus 20:5), perpetuating cycles of spiritual bondage until broken through prayer, repentance, and the authority of Christ.

7. Scriptural Perspective on Christians and Demons:

While some debate whether Christians can be affected by demonic influence, Scripture affirms the reality of spiritual warfare and admonishes believers to stand firm against the schemes of the devil (Ephesians 6:10-18). While believers possess authority over demonic forces in Christ's name (Luke 10:19), they must also exercise discernment and seek spiritual guidance when facing spiritual attacks.

Understanding our tripartite nature provides a framework for navigating the complexities of spiritual life, empowering believers to pursue holiness, freedom, and victory in Christ.

CHAPTER 15:

Unveiling the Power of Soul Ties and Soul Bonds

Soul ties and soul bonds are intricate spiritual connections that have profound implications on our lives, relationships, and spiritual well-being. Rooted in biblical principles, these connections shape our interactions and can either uplift or hinder our spiritual growth. Let's delve deeper into this topic, exploring its biblical foundation and practical applications.

1. Scriptural Insights into Soul Ties:

The Bible provides rich examples of soul ties, illustrating the depth of emotional and spiritual connections between individuals. In 1 Samuel 18:1, we witness the remarkable bond between David and Jonathan, where their souls were knit together in love and friendship. This narrative showcases the transformative power of soul connections, transcending mere human relationships.

2. The Concept of One Flesh:

The New Testament expands on the concept of soul ties through the principle of becoming one flesh in marriage and sexual union. In 1 Corinthians 6:16, Paul emphasizes the profound unity that occurs when individuals engage in sexual intimacy, highlighting the spiritual fusion that accompanies physical union. Similarly, in Mark 10:8, Jesus reinforces the notion of oneness in marriage, underscoring the spiritual and emotional bond that unites husband and wife.

3. Understanding Spiritual Oneness:

Soul ties extend beyond physical relationships, encompassing emotional and spiritual connections forged through friendships, partnerships, and shared experiences. These connections can be both godly and ungodly, influencing our thoughts, emotions, and spiritual well-being. Proverbs 27:17 reminds us of the impact of relationships: "Iron sharpens iron, and one man sharpens another." This verse underscores the transformative nature of soul connections, shaping our character and spiritual journey.

4. Breaking Ungodly Soul Ties:

While soul ties can foster intimacy and mutual support, ungodly connections can become avenues for spiritual oppression and demonic influence. Ephesians 6:12 reminds us that "we do not wrestle against flesh and blood, but against the rulers, against the authorities, against the cosmic powers over this present darkness." Therefore, breaking ungodly soul ties is essential for spiritual liberation and deliverance from demonic strongholds.

5. Principles of Spiritual Warfare:

Breaking ungodly soul ties requires spiritual discernment, prayer, and strategic warfare. 2 Corinthians 10:4-5 emphasizes the weapons of our warfare: "For the weapons of our warfare are not of the flesh but have divine power to destroy strongholds. We destroy arguments and every lofty opinion raised against the knowledge of God and take every thought captive to obey Christ." Through prayer, repentance, and renunciation, individuals can sever unhealthy spiritual connections and reclaim their spiritual autonomy.

6. Restoration and Healing:

Breaking ungodly soul ties is not merely about liberation from bondage but also about restoration and healing. Psalm 147:3 assures us of God's healing power: "He heals the brokenhearted and binds up their wounds." As individuals surrender their past hurts and brokenness to God, they can experience inner healing, renewal, and restoration of their spiritual identity.

7. Navigating Relationships with Wisdom:

Understanding the dynamics of soul ties equips believers to navigate their relationships with wisdom and discernment. Proverbs 4:23 admonishes us to "Above all else, guard your heart, for everything you do flows from it." By cultivating healthy boundaries, seeking godly counsel, and aligning with God's will, individuals can foster healthy relationships and guard against spiritual entanglements.

In conclusion, soul ties and soul bonds are intricate spiritual connections that shape our relationships and spiritual journey. By anchoring ourselves in biblical truths, engaging in strategic warfare, and seeking God's guidance, we can break free from ungodly soul ties, experience spiritual liberation, and walk in greater intimacy with our Heavenly Father.

Here's an example of a prayer to break an ungodly soul tie and bond:

"Heavenly Father, I come before you in the name of Jesus Christ, recognizing the power of soul ties and bonds in my life. I confess any ungodly connections I have formed with [name the person or situation], and I ask for your forgiveness and cleansing.

I renounce and break every ungodly soul tie and bond that I have formed with [name], whether through friendship, partnership, or past experiences. I declare that these soul ties are null and void in the name of Jesus.

I release [name] from any influence or control they have over my thoughts, emotions, or spiritual well-being. I sever every spiritual cord and connection that binds us together, and I command any demonic influence associated with these soul ties to leave my life now, in Jesus' mighty name.

Lord, I ask you to fill every void left by these broken soul ties with your love, peace, and Holy Spirit. Heal any wounds or hurts caused by these relationships and restore me to wholeness according to your perfect will.

I surrender my heart, mind, and spirit to you, Lord, and I pray for discernment and wisdom in all my relationships. Help me to guard my heart and walk in purity and obedience to your Word.

Thank you, Father, for your faithfulness and grace. I trust in your power to break every chain and set me free from the bondage of ungodly soul ties. In Jesus' name, I pray. Amen."

CHAPTER 16:

Forgiveness of Sin in Deliverance Ministry

Forgiveness lies at the heart of deliverance ministry, for it is through forgiveness that we break the chains of sin and oppression. In the journey of setting others free from demonic influence, understanding the profound significance of forgiveness is paramount.

Scriptural Foundation:

The Bible teaches us the transformative power of forgiveness. In Matthew 6:14-15, Jesus states, "For if you forgive other people when they sin against you, your heavenly Father will also forgive you. But if you do not forgive others their sins, your Father will not forgive your sins." This underscores the essential nature of forgiveness in the Christian faith.

Forgiveness in Deliverance:

In the context of deliverance ministry, forgiveness plays a dual role. Firstly, it is crucial for the one seeking deliverance to repent and seek forgiveness for any sins or open doors that have allowed demonic influence in their lives. This act of repentance opens the door for God's grace and deliverance to flow.

Secondly, forgiveness is often necessary towards others who may have wronged or hurt the individual seeking deliverance. Unforgiveness can serve as a barrier to freedom, as it can provide legal ground for demonic oppression. Releasing forgiveness is not only an act of obedience to God's command but also a strategic step towards breaking the chains of bondage.

Prayer of Forgiveness:

A prayer of forgiveness can be a powerful tool in deliverance ministry. Here's an example of a prayer:

"Heavenly Father, I come before you recognizing my need for forgiveness. I repent of every sin, known and unknown, that I have committed. I ask for your forgiveness and cleansing by the blood of Jesus Christ.

I also choose to forgive those who have wronged me. I release them from any debt they owe me, just as you have forgiven me. I choose to let go of bitterness, resentment, and unforgiveness, and I ask for your grace to heal my wounded heart.

Lord, I surrender every hurt, betrayal, and offense into your hands. I release any legal rights the enemy may have gained through unforgiveness, and I declare my freedom in Christ.

Thank you, Lord, for your mercy and grace. I receive your forgiveness and extend it to others, walking in the freedom and peace that comes from obedience to your Word. In Jesus' name, amen."

In deliverance ministry, forgiveness is not merely a suggestion but a vital component of spiritual warfare. As ministers of reconciliation, we carry the message of forgiveness and freedom, leading others into the transformative power of God's love and grace.

CHAPTER 17:

The Main Weapons
of Deliverance

In the battlefield of spiritual warfare, understanding the arsenal at our disposal is crucial. Each weapon serves a specific purpose and is instrumental in dismantling the enemy's strongholds. Let's explore the main weapons of deliverance and their effectiveness in combatting demonic forces.

1. The Cross: Symbolizing the triumph of Christ over Satan, the cross is a potent weapon against demonic entities. By invoking the power of the cross, demons are compelled to acknowledge their defeat and submit to the authority of Jesus Christ.

2. The Bible: The Word of God is described as sharper than any double-edged sword, capable of piercing through spiritual darkness and exposing the enemy's schemes. Utilizing scripture as a weapon, we confront demonic entities with truth and authority, dismantling their lies and strongholds.

3. Anointing Oil: Representing the presence and power of the Holy Spirit, anointing oil is employed to consecrate and

sanctify individuals and spaces for spiritual warfare. Its application often provokes demonic manifestations, signaling the presence of God's Spirit.

4. Salt: Inspired by Elisha's miraculous healing of water, salt symbolizes purification and protection against demonic influences. When used in deliverance ministry, salt serves as a symbol of God's covenant and authority, driving out unclean spirits and restoring spiritual purity.

5. Pulling out Body Parts: In the spiritual realm, demons experience pain and discomfort. By commanding the removal of demonic attributes such as fangs, claws, and scales in Jesus' name, we inflict spiritual warfare and weaken the enemy's grip on individuals.

6. Confusion: Just as God promised to throw confusion upon Israel's enemies, we invoke divine confusion to scatter demonic forces and disrupt their schemes. Confusion destabilizes the enemy's ranks, rendering them vulnerable to defeat.

7. Worship: Ascribing worth and honor to God weakens the enemy's hold on individuals and environments. By engaging in worship, we exalt the name of Jesus and diminish the influence of demonic entities, compelling them to flee in the presence of divine glory.

8. The Blood of Jesus: The blood of Jesus is the ultimate weapon against demonic forces, symbolizing redemption, and atonement. Demons tremble at the mention of the blood, acknowledging its power to cleanse and deliver.

9. Torment: Jesus's authority to torment demons before their appointed time reminds us of our authority to inflict torment upon demonic entities. By invoking divine torment, we disrupt the peace and comfort demons seek to establish, driving them out of their hiding places.

10. Angels: God's ministering spirits are dispatched to assist believers in spiritual warfare. By invoking the aid of angels in Jesus' name, we call upon heavenly reinforcements to combat demonic forces and enforce God's will on earth.

11. Music: Just as David's harp playing soothed King Saul's troubled spirit, music can have a profound impact on spiritual atmospheres. By engaging in worship through music, we create an environment conducive to God's presence, driving out demonic influences.

12. Breaking Ranks and Structure: Recognizing the hierarchical structure of demonic forces, we strategically target their ranks and divisions. By disrupting their organization and unity, we weaken their collective strength and facilitate their defeat.

13. Blessing: As vessels of God's blessing, we release divine favor and protection upon individuals, rendering them untouchable by demonic curses or attacks. Blessing serves as a shield against the enemy's schemes, fortifying believers in their spiritual warfare.

14. Test their Loyalty: Demons, characterized by their treachery and disloyalty, can be compelled to betray one another in exchange for leniency. By testing their loyalty and exploiting

their inherent deceitfulness, we extract valuable information and weaken their unity.

In conclusion, the arsenal of deliverance encompasses a diverse array of weapons, each tailored to address specific spiritual challenges and confront demonic opposition. By wielding these weapons with faith, authority, and strategic wisdom, we engage in spiritual warfare with confidence, knowing that victory is assured through Christ Jesus.

CHAPTER 18:

How to Put on the Armor of God

Introduction: The Armor of God

The Apostle Paul's exhortation to the Ephesian believers regarding the armor of God serves as a timeless blueprint for spiritual warfare. Penned during his imprisonment in Rome, Paul drew inspiration from the Roman guards who stood watch over him, using their physical armor as a metaphor for the spiritual protection needed by every follower of Christ. In a city rife with idolatry and spiritual warfare, Paul's words provided essential guidance to the Ephesian Christians and continue to resonate with believers today.

Ephesians 6:10-20: Christian Warfare

In Ephesians 6:10-20, Paul outlines the necessity of spiritual armor in combating the schemes of the devil. He emphasizes that our struggle is not against flesh and blood but against the spiritual forces of darkness. Therefore, believers are instructed to don the full armor of God to withstand the attacks of the enemy and stand firm in faith.

Helmet of Salvation

Scripture: Ephesians 6:17a - "Take the helmet of salvation..."

Expanding: The helmet of salvation signifies the assurance and confidence that comes from knowing we are saved by God's grace through faith in Jesus Christ. It protects our minds from doubts, fears, and the lies of the enemy, reminding us of our identity as redeemed children of God.

Breastplate of Righteousness

Scripture: Ephesians 6:14b - "...with the breastplate of righteousness in place..."

Expanding: The breastplate of righteousness represents the righteousness imputed to us through Christ's sacrifice. It guards our hearts against the accusations of the enemy and empowers us to live holy lives, standing firm in God's promises and resisting the allure of sin.

Shield of Faith

Scripture: Ephesians 6:16 - "In addition to all this, take up the shield of faith, with which you can extinguish all the flaming arrows of the evil one."

Expanding: The shield of faith serves as our defense against the enemy's attacks, deflecting the fiery darts of doubt, temptation, and deception. Grounded in God's promises, our faith enables us to remain steadfast and overcome every assault of the enemy.

Sword of the Spirit

Scripture: Ephesians 6:17 - "...and the sword of the Spirit, which is the word of God."

Expanding: The sword of the Spirit, the Word of God, is our offensive weapon in spiritual warfare. Just as Jesus wielded scripture to combat the devil's temptations, we use God's Word to expose falsehoods, proclaim truth, and defeat the enemy's schemes.

Belt of Truth

Scripture: Ephesians 6:14 - "Stand firm then, with the belt of truth buckled around your waist..."

Expanding: The belt of truth secures our spiritual armor and signifies our commitment to living in alignment with God's truth. It encompasses the Gospel message of redemption, our new identity in Christ, and a lifestyle characterized by honesty and integrity.

Shoes of the Gospel

Scripture: Ephesians 6:15 - "...and with your feet fitted with the readiness that comes from the gospel of peace."

Expanding: The shoes of the gospel equip us to share the Good News of Jesus Christ and advance His kingdom. They enable us to walk confidently in God's peace, demonstrating love for our neighbors, trusting in the Lord's provision, and spreading the message of salvation to a world in need.

As believers clothe themselves daily in the armor of God, they stand prepared to engage in spiritual warfare, knowing that victory is assured through the power of Christ.

The Devil's Armor

In Luke 11:21-22, Jesus speaks of a strong man armed, guarding his palace and possessions. However, when a stronger man overcomes him, he strips away the armor in which he trusted. This imagery portrays the tactics of Satan, who seeks to keep people bound in spiritual darkness through his own sinister armor, diametrically opposed to the protection offered by God.

Satan's Armor

Satan's armor serves to ensnare and deceive, fostering bondage and despair. These demonic implements stand in stark contrast to the armor of God and must be dismantled for true freedom to be attained.

The Helmet of Damnation

This insidious piece of Satan's armor plants seeds of doubt and convinces individuals that they are beyond redemption. It clouds the mind with thoughts of hopelessness, convincing them that salvation is unattainable.

The Breastplate of Sin

Designed to weigh down the heart with guilt and condemnation, the breastplate of sin reinforces the belief that one's sins are too great to be forgiven. It perpetuates a sense of unworthiness and separation from God's grace.

Shield of Fear

Contrary to the shield of faith, which offers protection and assurance, the shield of fear amplifies doubt and anxiety. It paralyzes believers, preventing them from stepping out in faith and trusting in God's promises.

Sword of Corruption

The sword of corruption distorts truth with lies, leading people astray and entangling them in deception. It perverts God's Word, sowing confusion and undermining the foundation of faith.

Belt of Lies

Functioning as a stronghold of falsehoods, the belt of lies entrenches false beliefs and distorts reality. It binds individuals to deceptive ideologies, hindering them from embracing the truth of God's Word.

The Shoes of the False Gospel

These deceptive footwear propagate counterfeit truths, masquerading as genuine gospel messages. They lead astray those who embrace them, steering them away from the path of salvation and into spiritual deception.

As believers engage in spiritual warfare, they must recognize and reject the devil's armor, relying instead on the unyielding protection of God's armor. Through prayer, discernment, and the wielding of God's Word, they can overcome the schemes of the enemy and walk in the victory secured by Christ.

Scriptures:

- Luke 11:21-22
- Ephesians 6:10-18

CHAPTER 19:

Breaking Demonic Blood Sacrifices and Covenants

In the intricate tapestry of spiritual warfare, the echoes of ancestral blood sacrifices and covenants reverberate across generations, casting dark shadows over the lives of descendants. Understanding the profound impact of these ancient rituals is paramount to breaking free from their oppressive grip and reclaiming spiritual freedom.

The Lingering Effects of Ancestral Blood Sacrifices

1. Generational Curses: Blood sacrifices performed by ancestors can establish generational curses that linger and afflict descendants. These curses, rooted in the shedding of innocent blood, create spiritual strongholds that perpetuate cycles of bondage, sickness, and misfortune within families.

2. Inherited Spiritual Bondage: The spiritual repercussions of ancestral blood sacrifices extend beyond mere curses, entangling descendants in webs of spiritual bondage. The demonic entities invoked through these rituals often latch

onto family bloodlines, exerting influence and control over successive generations.

3. Opening Spiritual Doors: Ancestral blood sacrifices serve as potent rituals that open spiritual doors to demonic forces, inviting them to wreak havoc and sow discord within family lines. These spiritual gateways provide malevolent entities with legal ground to afflict and oppress descendants, hindering their spiritual growth and well-being.

4. Sowing Seeds of Dysfunction: The spiritual defilement caused by ancestral blood sacrifices can manifest in various forms of dysfunction within families, including addiction, mental illness, and relational strife. These patterns of dysfunction often trace their origins back to the spiritual contamination inherited from past generations.

Breaking the Chains of Ancestral Bondage

1. Identification and Renunciation: Acknowledging and renouncing the spiritual ties to ancestral blood sacrifices is the first step toward breaking free from their grip. Descendants must recognize the spiritual inheritance they have received and consciously sever these unholy bonds through prayer and repentance.

2. Repentance and Restoration: Engaging in heartfelt repentance on behalf of ancestral sins and bloodshed is essential for breaking generational curses and restoring spiritual purity. By humbling themselves before God and seeking His forgiveness, descendants can initiate the process of spiritual restoration and deliverance.

3. 3. Covering in the Blood of Jesus: The blood of Jesus Christ is the ultimate cleansing agent that has the power to wash away the defilement of ancestral blood sacrifices. Through faith in the redemptive work of Christ, descendants can appropriate His blood to break every curse, dissolve every covenant, and release themselves from spiritual bondage.

4. 4. Walking in Authority: Armed with the authority bestowed upon them as children of God, descendants can actively engage in spiritual warfare to dismantle the strongholds erected by ancestral blood sacrifices. By standing firm in their identity in Christ and wielding the spiritual weapons at their disposal, they can enforce freedom and deliverance over their bloodlines.

Conclusion

The legacy of ancestral blood sacrifices is a dark stain on the tapestry of family history, but it need not define the destiny of descendants. Through repentance, faith, and spiritual warfare, individuals can break free from the chains of ancestral bondage, reclaim their spiritual inheritance, and walk in the fullness of God's freedom and blessing.

Scriptures:

- Exodus 34:7
- Deuteronomy 23:2
- Psalm 79:3
- 1 Peter 1:18-19
- Colossians 1:13-14

Prayer to Break Demonic Sacrifices and Covenants:

Example Prayer:

Heavenly Father,

I come before You in the mighty name of Jesus Christ, acknowledging Your sovereignty over all spiritual forces and realms. I repent on behalf of myself, my ancestors, and my bloodline for any participation in or connection to demonic sacrifices, blood covenants, or occult rituals that have been performed knowingly or unknowingly.

I renounce and reject every covenant, pact, or agreement made with the forces of darkness through blood sacrifices or any other means. I declare that I am covered by the blood of Jesus Christ, and no curse or covenant formed against me shall prosper.

By the authority given to me as a child of God, I break every generational curse, spiritual stronghold, and demonic bondage established through ancestral blood sacrifices. I command every demonic entity associated with these sacrifices to leave my life, my family, and my bloodline now, in the name of Jesus.

I plead the blood of Jesus over every aspect of my being—spirit, soul, and body—cleansing me from all defilement and releasing me from every spiritual entanglement. I declare my allegiance to Jesus Christ and His kingdom, and I submit myself fully to His lordship and authority.

I declare that I am free from the consequences of ancestral blood sacrifices and covenants, and I walk in the liberty and victory purchased for me by the sacrifice of Jesus Christ on the cross. I thank You, Lord, for Your deliverance and restoration in my life, and I receive Your grace to walk in freedom and victory each day.

In Jesus' name, I pray. Amen.

CHAPTER 20:

The Importance
of Binding Demons
in Spiritual Warfare

In the realm of spiritual warfare, binding demons is a crucial aspect of confronting and overcoming the forces of darkness. Understanding the significance of binding demons empowers believers to exercise their authority in Christ effectively and dismantle the works of the enemy.

1. Authority in Christ: Binding demons is rooted in the authority given to believers by Jesus Christ Himself. In Luke 10:19, Jesus says, "Behold, I give you the authority to trample on serpents and scorpions, and over all the power of the enemy, and nothing shall by any means hurt you." This authority enables believers to restrain and render ineffective the activities of demonic entities.

2. Blocking Satanic Influence: Binding demons prevents them from carrying out their malicious plans and assignments. By binding them in the name of Jesus, believers cut off their ability to manipulate circumstances, hinder God's work, and

afflict individuals with spiritual oppression, sickness, or bondage.

3. Protecting Individuals and Environments: Binding demons safeguards individuals, families, communities, and territories from spiritual attacks and influences. It creates a spiritual barrier that shields against demonic intrusion, ensuring peace, safety, and spiritual freedom in the lives of believers and their surroundings.

4. Releasing God's Purposes: Binding demons aligns with God's desire to establish His kingdom and manifest His glory on earth. By restraining demonic activity, believers pave the way for God's purposes to be fulfilled, allowing His light to shine brightly and His will to be accomplished in people's lives and in the world.

5. Intercession and Spiritual Warfare: Binding demons is an essential component of intercessory prayer and spiritual warfare. Believers engage in strategic prayer by binding demonic strongholds, hindrances, and principalities that oppose God's plans, thereby clearing the path for His kingdom to advance and His blessings to flow unhindered.

6. Victory in Christ: Binding demons reinforces the truth of believers' victory in Christ. As stated in Colossians 2:15, Jesus "disarmed principalities and powers" through His death and resurrection, triumphing over them openly. By binding demons, believers enforce this victory and proclaim Christ's authority over all spiritual forces.

In conclusion, binding demons is a potent spiritual weapon that believers wield in their warfare against the kingdom of darkness.

It demonstrates faith in Christ's authority, blocks satanic influence, protects individuals and environments, releases God's purposes, facilitates intercession, and affirms victory in Christ. As believers exercise their authority in binding demons, they participate in God's redemptive work and advance His kingdom on earth.

Example Prayer to Bind Demons:

"Heavenly Father, I come before You in the name of Jesus Christ, my Savior and Redeemer. I acknowledge Your sovereignty and authority over all creation, including the spiritual realm. I thank You for the victory won for me through the death and resurrection of Your Son, Jesus Christ.

In accordance with Your Word and the authority given to me as a believer in Christ, I now take authority over every demonic spirit that seeks to hinder, oppress, or afflict me or anyone else. I bind every spirit of darkness, every principality, power, ruler of the darkness of this world, and spiritual wickedness in high places, in the mighty name of Jesus.

I command every demonic force operating in my life, my family, my home, and my environment to be bound and rendered powerless. I break every assignment, plot, and scheme of the enemy against me, and I cancel every demonic contract or covenant made against me or my loved ones.

I cover myself, my family, and my possessions with the precious blood of Jesus, and I declare that no weapon formed against us shall prosper. I decree and declare the protection of Your holy angels around us, guarding us from all harm and danger.

I release the fire of the Holy Spirit to consume every demonic stronghold, every evil altar, and every source of spiritual contamination in my life and surroundings. I command every demon to flee and to never return, in the name of Jesus.

Father, I thank You for Your faithfulness and Your promise to hear and answer the prayers of Your children. I trust in Your power and Your love to deliver me from every attack of the enemy and to keep me safe in Your hands.

I declare this prayer to be effective and I seal it with the authority of Jesus Christ, amen."

CHAPTER 21:

Renouncing Idolatry
and its Effects on
a Christian

Introduction:

Idolatry, throughout history, has been one of the most prevalent sins among humanity. It involves the worship of anything other than the one true God. In today's context, idolatry can take many forms beyond statues and carved images. It can be the pursuit of material possessions, fame, power, or even the elevation of relationships above God. For Christians, idolatry poses a significant threat to their spiritual well-being and relationship with God. In this chapter, we will explore the importance of renouncing idolatry and the profound effects it can have on a Christian's life.

Understanding Idolatry:

Idolatry is not just bowing down to physical idols but also involves placing anything or anyone above God in our lives. It could be our careers, relationships, possessions, or even our own desires and ambitions. The Bible is clear in its condemnation of idolatry, recognizing it as a violation of the first commandment (Exodus 20:3-5) and warning against its allure and consequences (1 Corinthians 10:14).

Effects of Idolatry on a Christian:

1. Spiritual Bondage: Idolatry enslaves the heart and mind, leading to spiritual bondage and separation from God. When we prioritize anything above God, we become enslaved to those desires or pursuits, hindering our intimacy with Him.

2. Loss of Discernment: Idolatry clouds our spiritual discernment, making it difficult to distinguish between God's will and our selfish desires. It distorts our perception of truth and leads us astray from God's purposes for our lives.

3. Broken Fellowship with God: Idolatry erects barriers between us and God, hindering our ability to experience His presence and receive His blessings. It disrupts our fellowship with Him, leaving us spiritually empty and discontented.

4. Moral Decay: Idolatry often leads to moral decay as we compromise our values and principles in pursuit of worldly pleasures or ambitions. It can result in unethical behavior, addiction, and a gradual erosion of our moral integrity.

5. Spiritual Dryness: Engaging in idolatrous practices can result in spiritual dryness and stagnation. Instead of finding fulfillment and satisfaction, we experience emptiness and dissatisfaction, as idols fail to fulfill the deep longing of our souls.

Renouncing Idolatry:

Renouncing idolatry begins with acknowledging its presence in our lives and its detrimental effects on our relationship with God. It requires a sincere repentance and turning away from anything that competes with God for our affection and allegiance. Renouncing idolatry involves:

1. Confession: Confessing our involvement in idolatrous practices and acknowledging them as sin before God.

2. Repentance: Turning away from idolatry and committing to seek God's kingdom and righteousness above all else.

3. Surrender: Surrendering every area of our lives to God's lordship and allowing Him to reign supreme in our hearts.

4. Cleansing: Seeking God's forgiveness and cleansing from the defilement of idolatry through the blood of Jesus Christ.

5. Renewal: Embracing a renewed mind and spirit, focused on glorifying God and living in obedience to His word.

Conclusion:

Renouncing idolatry is essential for every Christian who desires to walk closely with God and experience the fullness of His blessings. It requires a deliberate choice to prioritize God above all else and to guard our hearts against the subtle allure of worldly idols. As we renounce idolatry and pursue whole-hearted devotion to God, we will find true fulfillment, joy, and satisfaction in Him alone.

Example Prayer:

Heavenly Father,

I come before you with a humble heart, recognizing the sin of idolatry that has crept into my life. I confess that at times I have placed other things and desires above You, seeking fulfillment and satisfaction in the created rather than the Creator. Lord, forgive me for my idolatry, for the times I have worshiped false gods and pursued worldly pleasures instead of seeking Your will.

I renounce every form of idolatry in my life, whether it be the love of money, success, relationships, or any other pursuit that has taken precedence over my love and devotion to You. I declare that You alone are worthy of my worship and allegiance, and I surrender every area of my life to Your lordship.

I repent of the times I have allowed idols to take root in my heart, and I ask for Your cleansing and forgiveness. Wash me clean with the blood of Jesus and purify me from all unrighteousness. Help me to turn away from idolatrous practices and to set my affection on things above, where Christ is seated at Your right hand.

Fill me afresh with Your Holy Spirit, that I may walk in obedience to Your word and live a life that glorifies You in all things. Grant me the strength to resist the temptations of idolatry and to remain steadfast in my devotion to You.

I thank You, Lord, for Your mercy and grace, and for the freedom I have in Christ to renounce idolatry and live as a child of God. May Your name be exalted above every idol in my life, now and forevermore. In Jesus' name, I pray, Amen.

CHAPTER 22:

Renouncing Witchcraft, Sorcery, and Divination
in Deliverance Ministry

Introduction:

In the realm of deliverance ministry, confronting and renouncing witchcraft, sorcery, and divination are critical components of spiritual warfare. These practices, rooted in rebellion against God and seeking power apart from Him, can have profound spiritual implications for individuals and communities. This chapter will delve into the significance of renouncing witchcraft, sorcery, and divination within the context of deliverance ministry.

Understanding Witchcraft, Sorcery, and Divination:

1. Witchcraft: Witchcraft involves the use of supernatural powers or rituals to influence events or people according to one's will. It often includes the invocation of spirits, casting spells, or performing rituals to manipulate outcomes.

2. Sorcery: Sorcery is the practice of using magic or enchantments to control or harm others. It may involve the use of potions, charms, or rituals to achieve desired effects, often at the expense of others' well-being.

3. Divination: Divination is the attempt to gain insight or foretell the future through supernatural means. This can include practices such as tarot card reading, astrology, or seeking guidance from spiritual entities outside of God.

The Significance of Renunciation:

1. Breaking Spiritual Bondage: Renouncing witchcraft, sorcery, and divination is essential for breaking spiritual bondage and freeing individuals from demonic influence and oppression.

2. Closing Doors to the Enemy: Renunciation closes the doors that were opened through involvement in these practices, depriving the enemy of legal ground to operate in a person's life.

3. Repentance and Restoration: Renunciation is a crucial step in the process of repentance and restoration, allowing individuals to turn away from sinful practices and align themselves with God's will.

4. Spiritual Cleansing: Renouncing witchcraft, sorcery, and divination facilitates spiritual cleansing and purification, removing the defilement associated with these practices and restoring spiritual purity.

5. Protection and Deliverance: Renunciation opens the door for God's protection and deliverance, enabling individuals to walk in freedom and victory over the forces of darkness.

The Process of Renunciation in Deliverance Ministry:

1. Identification: Identify any involvement with witchcraft, sorcery, or divination through personal reflection, confession, and prayer. Seek the guidance of the Holy Spirit to uncover hidden areas of bondage.

2. Confession and Repentance: Confess and repent of any participation in witchcraft, sorcery, or divination, acknowledging these practices as sin and turning away from them with a contrite heart.

3. Renunciation: Verbally renounce witchcraft, sorcery, and divination, declaring your rejection of these practices and your commitment to follow God wholeheartedly.

4. Breaking Soul Ties and Covenants: Break any soul ties or covenants formed through involvement in witchcraft, sorcery, or divination, declaring their nullification in the name of Jesus Christ.

5. Prayer of Deliverance: Pray for deliverance from any demonic influence or oppression associated with these practices, invoking the power of Jesus' name to bind and cast out every spirit of witchcraft, sorcery, and divination.

Conclusion:

Renouncing witchcraft, sorcery, and divination is a vital aspect of deliverance ministry, enabling individuals to break free from spiritual bondage and walk in the freedom and victory that Christ has provided. Through confession, repentance, and renunciation, individuals can experience cleansing, restoration, and deliverance, allowing them to live in alignment with God's will and purposes for their lives.

Example Prayer:

Heavenly Father,

I come before you in the name of Jesus Christ, acknowledging that You are the only true and living God, and there is no power greater than Yours. I confess that I have been involved in practices of witchcraft, sorcery, and divination, knowingly or unknowingly, and I repent of these sins with a sincere heart.

I renounce every form of witchcraft, including the use of spells, charms, potions, and rituals to manipulate or control people or circumstances. I reject the lure of sorcery, which seeks to harness supernatural powers for personal gain or harm. I turn away from divination, which relies on occult practices to seek knowledge or insight apart from You, O Lord.

I declare that I am no longer under the bondage of witchcraft, sorcery, or divination. I break every soul tie and covenant formed through my involvement in these practices, and I nullify their influence over my life by the authority of Jesus Christ.

In the name of Jesus, I command every demonic spirit associated with witchcraft, sorcery, and divination to leave me now and go to the feet of Jesus for judgment. I bind and rebuke every evil force that has sought to ensnare me through these practices, and I declare my freedom in Christ.

Fill me, Lord, with Your Holy Spirit and cover me with the precious blood of Jesus. Cleanse me from all unrighteousness and purify me from every defilement of witchcraft. Help me to walk in obedience to Your Word and to trust in Your power alone.

Thank You, Father, for Your forgiveness, Your deliverance, and Your love. I surrender my life to You completely and commit to following You wholeheartedly from this day forward. In Jesus' mighty name, I pray. Amen.

CHAPTER 23:

The Effects of Witchcraft, Sorcery, and Divination on a Christian

Introduction:

Witchcraft, sorcery, and divination are practices explicitly forbidden by God in the Bible. Despite this, many Christians, knowingly or unknowingly, dabble in these occult activities, often under the guise of harmless curiosity or seeking supernatural insight. However, the consequences of involvement in witchcraft, sorcery, and divination can be profound and far-reaching, affecting every aspect of a believer's life.

Effects of Witchcraft, Sorcery, and Divination:

1. Spiritual Bondage: Engaging in witchcraft, sorcery, or divination opens doors to demonic influence and oppression. These practices involve invoking spiritual forces outside of God, thereby allowing demonic entities to gain access and exert control over a Christian's life.

2. Mental and Emotional Turmoil: Participation in occult activities can lead to confusion, anxiety, and emotional instability. Demonic spirits associated with witchcraft and sorcery often torment individuals with intrusive thoughts, irrational fears, and psychological distress.

3. Physical Afflictions: Witchcraft, sorcery, and divination can manifest in physical ailments and unexplained illnesses. Demons invoked through occult practices may cause bodily harm, chronic pain, and various health issues as a means of exerting their influence over the believer.

4. Strained Relationships: The presence of demonic influences resulting from involvement in witchcraft, sorcery, or divination can disrupt and damage interpersonal relationships. Demonic spirits may sow discord, suspicion, and conflict among family members, friends, and church communities.

5. Spiritual Stagnation: Instead of seeking guidance and empowerment from God, individuals involved in witchcraft, sorcery, or divination may rely on occult practices for direction and empowerment. This reliance on forbidden spiritual sources hinders spiritual growth and intimacy with God.

6. Legal and Financial Challenges: The consequences of engaging in occult practices may extend to legal and financial realms. Demonic oppression resulting from involvement in witchcraft, sorcery, or divination can lead to legal troubles, financial loss, and hindrances in career or business endeavors.

7. Loss of Discernment: Regular participation in witchcraft, sorcery, or divination can dull a Christian's ability to discern between truth and deception. The enemy may deceive individuals into believing falsehoods, leading them away from God's Word and His will for their lives.

Conclusion:

The effects of witchcraft, sorcery, and divination on a Christian are profound and detrimental to spiritual, emotional, physical, and relational well-being. It is crucial for believers to renounce these practices, seek deliverance from demonic influences, and turn wholeheartedly to God for forgiveness, healing, and restoration. By aligning their lives with God's Word and relying on His power, Christians can overcome the effects of occult involvement and walk in freedom and victory in Christ.

CHAPTER 24:

The Importance of Breaking Curses, Spells, Hexes, and Vexes in Deliverance Ministry

Introduction:

Curses, spells, hexes, and vexes are malevolent spiritual forces employed by practitioners of witchcraft, sorcery, and occultism to bring harm, misfortune, and suffering upon individuals. These dark arts are wielded with the intent to manipulate, control, and inflict damage on the lives of others. In the realm of deliverance ministry, breaking curses and dispelling evil spells is of paramount importance to release individuals from the bondage and oppression imposed by these diabolical influences.

The Significance of Breaking Curses, Spells, Hexes, and Vexes:

1. Liberation from Spiritual Bondage: Curses and spells are often used by occult practitioners to ensnare individuals in spiritual bondage. Breaking these curses is essential to free individuals from the oppressive grip of malevolent forces and restore their spiritual autonomy and freedom in Christ.

2. Restoration of Blessings: Curses and spells have the power to obstruct God's blessings and prosperity in the lives of believers. By breaking these curses, individuals can reclaim God's promises of abundance, favor, and divine protection over their lives.

3. Healing and Wholeness: Curses and spells can manifest in physical ailments, emotional wounds, and psychological distress. Breaking these curses is a crucial step in facilitating inner healing, emotional restoration, and overall well-being in individuals who have been afflicted by malevolent spiritual forces.

4. Reversal of Negative Effects: Curses, spells, hexes, and vexes can bring about a myriad of negative effects, including financial setbacks, relationship conflicts, and career obstacles. Breaking these curses is instrumental in reversing these adverse effects and restoring individuals to a position of strength, resilience, and success.

5. Protection and Prevention: Breaking curses is not only about remedying existing afflictions but also about preventing future attacks and vulnerabilities to spiritual warfare. Through strategic prayer and spiritual warfare, individuals can fortify themselves against the schemes of the enemy and safeguard their lives from further demonic incursions.

6. Spiritual Warfare and Authority: Breaking curses requires exercising the spiritual authority bestowed upon believers by Christ. By invoking the name of Jesus and the power of His shed blood, believers can confront and dismantle curses,

spells, hexes, and vexes with confidence and efficacy, knowing that they have been granted authority over all the powers of darkness.

Conclusion:

In the realm of deliverance ministry, breaking curses, spells, hexes, and vexes is an indispensable component of spiritual warfare and liberation. It is through the fervent prayers, intercession, and faith of believers that individuals can be released from the grip of demonic oppression and restored to a position of victory and freedom in Christ. By recognizing the significance of breaking curses and wielding the authority granted to them by God, believers can effectively combat the forces of darkness and usher in God's kingdom of light, love, and redemption.

Example Prayer:

Heavenly Father,

I come before you in the mighty name of Jesus, acknowledging Your sovereignty and authority over all things. I stand on Your promises of deliverance and victory, knowing that You are greater than any curse, spell, hex, or vex that may be affecting my life.

I confess any sins or open doors in my life and the lives of my ancestors that may have allowed these curses and spells to take hold. I renounce any involvement in witchcraft, sorcery, or occult practices, and I repent of any rebellion or disobedience against Your commandments.

In the name of Jesus, I break every curse, spell, hex, and vex that has been spoken or sent against me, whether knowingly or unknowingly. I declare that these curses are null and void, for I am covered by the blood of Jesus and His victory on the cross.

I command every evil spirit associated with these curses to leave me now and go to the feet of Jesus for judgment. I bind the powers of darkness that have been oppressing me and command them to release their hold over my life, my family, my relationships, and my circumstances.

Lord, I ask for Your divine protection and covering over me and my loved ones. Fill us with Your Holy Spirit and surround us with Your angels, that we may be shielded from any further attacks of the enemy.

I declare Your Word over my life, that no weapon formed against me shall prosper, and every tongue that rises against me in judgment shall be condemned. I walk in the authority and power of Jesus Christ, knowing that You have given me victory over the forces of darkness.

Thank You, Lord, for Your faithfulness and Your deliverance. I receive Your freedom, Your peace, and Your abundant life, knowing that nothing can separate me from Your love.

In Jesus' name, amen.

CHAPTER 25:

The Effects of
Ancestral Sin on the Current Generation

Ancestral sin refers to the sinful actions, behaviors, and patterns of our ancestors that have lasting consequences on future generations. The Bible provides insight into the impact of ancestral sin on individuals and societies, shedding light on how these inherited patterns can influence our lives today.

1. Biblical Understanding of Ancestral Sin:

- Exodus 34:7: God reveals Himself as a God who visits the iniquity of the fathers upon the children to the third and fourth generations.
- Deuteronomy 5:9: God warns against idolatry, stating that He will punish the children for the sin of the parents to the third and fourth generation.
- Ezekiel 18:20: While individuals are responsible for their own sins, there is acknowledgment of the consequences of ancestral sin affecting future generations.

2. Generational Curses:

- Generational curses are believed to be the result of ancestral sin, passed down through family lines and manifesting as patterns of dysfunction, illness, and spiritual oppression.
- These curses can affect various aspects of life, including health, relationships, finances, and spiritual well-being.

3. Patterns of Sin and Behavior:

- Ancestral sin can perpetuate patterns of sinful behavior within families, such as addiction, abuse, dishonesty, and immorality.
- These patterns may be learned and passed down from one generation to another, shaping the worldview and values of individuals within the family.

4. Spiritual Strongholds:

- Ancestral sin can create spiritual strongholds, making it difficult for individuals to break free from sinful habits and patterns.
- These strongholds may give rise to spiritual oppression, bondage, and resistance to spiritual growth and transformation.

5. Healing and Restoration:

- While the effects of ancestral sin can be profound, the Bible also offers hope for healing and restoration.

- Through repentance, forgiveness, and faith in Jesus Christ, individuals can break free from the cycle of ancestral sin and experience spiritual liberation.
- Prayer, deliverance ministry, and seeking God's guidance are essential steps in overcoming generational curses and experiencing God's healing and transformation.

In conclusion, the Bible highlights the reality of ancestral sin and its effects on current generations. However, it also emphasizes the power of God's grace and redemption to break the chains of generational curses and bring healing and restoration to individuals and families. Through faith in Jesus Christ and obedience to His Word, we can overcome the impact of ancestral sin and walk in the freedom and abundant life that God intends for us.

Example Prayer:

Heavenly Father,

I come before You humbly, acknowledging the reality of ancestral sin and its effects on my life and the lives of my family members. I confess that the sins of my ancestors have influenced me in ways I may not fully understand, and I recognize the need to break free from these generational patterns.

Lord, I renounce and repent of every sin committed by my ancestors, known and unknown, that has had a negative impact on my life. I ask for Your forgiveness and cleansing from the consequences of these sins, and I thank You for Your mercy and grace.

I renounce every generational curse, stronghold, and pattern of sin that has been passed down through my family line. I break every chain that binds me to the sins of the past, and I declare my freedom in Christ.

I renounce any involvement in idolatry, witchcraft, sorcery, divination, or any other form of occult practice that may have been present in my family history. I sever all ties with these practices and declare my allegiance to You, Lord Jesus.

I ask You, Lord, to break every curse, spell, hex, and vex that has been spoken against me or my family members. I declare that no weapon formed against us shall prosper, and I claim victory in Your name.

I invite Your Holy Spirit to come and cleanse me from all unrighteousness, filling me with Your love, peace, and truth. Help me to walk in obedience to Your Word and to live a life that honors You in every way.

Thank You, Lord, for Your faithfulness and Your promise of freedom in Christ. May Your healing and restoration flow through my life and my family, breaking the power of ancestral sin and bringing forth abundant life in You.

In Jesus' name, I pray,
Amen.

CHAPTER 26:

The Biblical Significance of Renouncing Ancestral Actions, Consecrations, and Dedications Made on the Bloodline

In the realm of deliverance ministry, an essential aspect often arises – the acknowledgment of the spiritual implications stemming from the actions of our forebears. Across generations, families have engaged in covenants, oaths, and dedications, the effects of which reverberate through time. Understanding and addressing these ancestral ties are paramount for experiencing true freedom and restoration in Christ.

1. Recognition of Ancestral Actions:

It is imperative to recognize that our ancestors may have engaged in practices or agreements with spiritual entities contrary to God's will. These actions could encompass involvement in occult rituals, idol worship, or pledges made to false deities.

Deuteronomy 18:9-12 warns against such practices: "When you come into the land that the Lord your God is giving you, you shall not learn to follow the abominable practices of those nations... For whoever does these things is an abomination to the Lord."

2. Spiritual Inheritance:

Just as physical traits are passed down through generations, so too are spiritual predispositions. These inheritances may manifest as generational curses, sinful patterns, or spiritual strongholds impacting our lives today. Recognizing this inheritance is pivotal for breaking its hold.

Exodus 34:7 highlights the transmission of consequences: "Yet he does not leave the guilty unpunished; he punishes the children and their children for the sin of the parents to the third and fourth generation."

3. Renunciation and Repentance:

Renouncing the actions of our ancestors involves openly acknowledging and rejecting any agreements or covenants contrary to God's Word. This renunciation is accompanied by genuine repentance, turning away from past sins and aligning ourselves with God's truth.

Acts 3:19 underscores the importance of repentance: "Repent, then, and turn to God, so that your sins may be wiped out, that times of refreshing may come from the Lord."

4. Consecration to God:

Through renouncing ancestral ties, we consecrate ourselves to God's service, surrendering our will and desires to His divine purposes. This consecration entails a continual yielding to the Holy Spirit's work in our lives, striving for holiness and obedience.

Romans 12:1 exhorts believers to consecrate themselves: "Therefore, I urge you, brothers and sisters, in view of God's mercy, to offer your bodies as a living sacrifice, holy and pleasing to God — this is your true and proper worship."

5. Breaking Generational Curses:

Through renunciation and consecration, we break the power of generational curses that have ensnared our bloodline. These curses, whether manifested as illness, poverty, addiction, or dysfunction, lose their hold in the face of Christ's authority and the cleansing power of His blood.

Galatians 3:13 assures believers of Christ's redemption: "Christ redeemed us from the curse of the law by becoming a curse for us."

6. Restoration and Redemption:

Renouncing ancestral ties and consecrating ourselves to God opens the door to His healing and restoration. God's promise of redemption extends to every generation, breaking chains of bondage and bringing wholeness to our families.

Joel 2:25-26 speaks of God's restorative power: "I will repay you for the years the locusts have eaten... You will have plenty to eat, until you are full, and you will praise the name of the Lord your God."

7. Continual Vigilance:

Renouncing ancestral ties is an ongoing process requiring vigilance against the subtle influences of the past. Regular prayer, Scripture meditation, and fellowship with believers are vital for spiritual growth and maturity.

1 Peter 5:8 admonishes believers to be vigilant: "Be alert and of sober mind. Your enemy the devil prowls around like a roaring lion looking for someone to devour."

In conclusion, the importance of renouncing ancestral ties and consecrating ourselves to God cannot be overstated. It is a crucial step toward experiencing genuine freedom, healing, and restoration in Christ. Through renunciation and consecration, we break the power of generational curses and open the door to God's redemptive work in our lives and the lives of future generations.

Here's an example prayer to break ancestral consecrations and dedications:

"Heavenly Father, I come before you in the name of Jesus Christ, acknowledging the power and authority of your Son, who has conquered sin and death. I thank you for your love and mercy that extends to all generations, and I come seeking freedom and deliverance from any ancestral consecrations or dedications that have bound my family line.

I confess and renounce any oaths, covenants, or dedications made by my ancestors to false gods, idols, or spiritual entities that are contrary to your will and word. I repent of any participation in occult practices, idol worship, or rituals that have defiled my family line and opened doors to spiritual bondage.

In the name of Jesus, I break every ungodly covenant, oath, or dedication that has been made on behalf of my ancestors, whether knowingly or unknowingly. I declare that these agreements are null and void in the spiritual realm, and I revoke any legal rights that the enemy may have gained through them.

I consecrate myself and my family line to you, Lord, dedicating our lives wholly to your service and surrendering all areas of our hearts, minds, and spirits to your will. I ask for your forgiveness and cleansing, washing away every stain of sin and defilement with the precious blood of Jesus.

By the power of the Holy Spirit, I command every demonic influence associated with ancestral consecrations and dedications to be expelled from my life and family line. I break the chains of bondage and declare freedom and release in Jesus' name.

I plead the blood of Jesus over my family line, covering us with your protection and sealing us with your love. Let your light shine into every dark corner of our history, bringing healing, restoration, and redemption.

Thank you, Lord, for your faithfulness and grace. I receive your freedom and deliverance with gratitude and faith, trusting in your promises to restore what the enemy has stolen and to bring beauty from ashes. In Jesus' mighty name, amen."

CHAPTER 27:

Renouncing Satan
and Resisting Him in Deliverance Ministry

In the journey of deliverance ministry, one of the fundamental principles is the recognition of the reality of spiritual warfare and the role of Satan in orchestrating evil against humanity. Satan, also known as the devil, is a powerful adversary who seeks to steal, kill, and destroy (John 10:10). However, as believers in Christ, we have been given authority over the enemy, and part of our spiritual warfare involves renouncing Satan and resisting his schemes.

1. The Reality of Spiritual Warfare:

The Bible makes it clear that we are engaged in a spiritual battle against principalities, powers, and spiritual forces of evil (Ephesians 6:12). Satan and his demonic forces operate in the unseen realm, seeking to deceive, oppress, and hinder God's people.

2. Renouncing Satan:

Renouncing Satan involves openly acknowledging and rejecting his authority and influence in our lives. It is a conscious decision to break any ties or agreements we may have made with the enemy knowingly or unknowingly. Renunciation is accompanied by genuine repentance and a commitment to follow Christ wholeheartedly.

3. Resisting the Devil:

The Bible instructs us to resist the devil, and he will flee from us (James 4:7). Resisting the devil involves actively opposing his lies, temptations, and attacks with the truth of God's Word and the power of the Holy Spirit. It is a stance of defiance against the enemy's attempts to undermine our faith and obedience to God.

4. The Importance of Resistance in Deliverance Ministry:

In deliverance ministry, resisting the devil is crucial for achieving lasting freedom and victory over spiritual bondage. It is not enough to cast out demons; we must also close the door to their return by resisting the devil and his influence in our lives.

5. Standing Firm in Faith:

Resisting the devil requires standing firm in our faith in Christ and the authority we have been given as believers. We must rely on the promises of God's Word and the indwelling power of the Holy Spirit to overcome the enemy's attacks.

6. Putting on the Armor of God:

Ephesians 6:10-18 describes the spiritual armor that God has provided for believers to stand against the schemes of the devil. By putting on the armor of God, including the belt of truth, the breastplate of righteousness, the shield of faith, the helmet of salvation, and the sword of the Spirit, we can effectively resist the enemy's tactics.

7. Perseverance in Prayer:

Prayer is a powerful weapon in spiritual warfare, and we are instructed to pray at all times in the Spirit (Ephesians 6:18). Through prayer, we can seek God's protection, guidance, and strength to resist the devil and stand firm in our faith.

In conclusion, renouncing Satan and resisting him are essential aspects of deliverance ministry. As we acknowledge the reality of spiritual warfare, put on the armor of God, and stand firm in faith, we can experience victory over the enemy's schemes and walk in the freedom and authority that Christ has provided for us.

Example of Prayer:

Heavenly Father,

I come before you in the name of Jesus Christ, my Savior and Lord. I acknowledge that Satan is a defeated foe and has no authority over my life. I renounce any agreements, covenants, or ties I may have with him or his kingdom. I repent of any sin or rebellion that has given him a foothold in my life.

I declare that Jesus Christ is my Lord and King, and I submit myself fully to His authority. I resist the devil and all his works, including deception, temptation, oppression, and every form of evil. I take authority over every demonic influence and command them to leave me now in the name of Jesus.

I put on the whole armor of God – the belt of truth, the breastplate of righteousness, the shield of faith, the helmet of salvation, and the sword of the Spirit – and I stand firm against the enemy's attacks. I declare that no weapon formed against me shall prosper, and every tongue that rises against me in judgment shall be condemned.

I thank you, Lord, for your protection and deliverance. I trust in your promises and your power to overcome the enemy. Fill me afresh with your Holy Spirit and lead me in the paths of righteousness all the days of my life.

In Jesus' name, I pray. Amen.

CHAPTER 28:

Breaking Strongholds
in Deliverance Ministry

In the realm of spiritual warfare, strongholds are areas of entrenched spiritual resistance that hinder the work of God in our lives. These strongholds can manifest as deeply ingrained patterns of sin, persistent negative thoughts and beliefs, or areas of bondage that seem unbreakable. However, through the power of Christ, these strongholds can be torn down, and freedom can be found.

1. Identifying Strongholds:

Strongholds often originate from traumatic experiences, unaddressed sin, generational curses, or demonic oppression. They can manifest in various forms, such as addiction, fear, anger, unforgiveness, or pride. Identifying the specific strongholds in our lives is the first step toward breaking free from their grip.

2. Spiritual Weapons:

We cannot overcome strongholds through human effort alone; we need spiritual weapons. These include prayer, fasting, Scripture meditation, worship, confession, and the power of the Holy Spirit. By engaging in spiritual disciplines and relying on God's strength, we can effectively combat strongholds.

3. Renunciation and Repentance:

Breaking strongholds begins with renouncing any agreement with the enemy and repenting of sin. We must acknowledge the areas of our lives where we have allowed the enemy to gain a foothold and actively turn away from those behaviors. This act of renunciation and repentance is crucial for dismantling strongholds.

4. Prayer and Intercession:

Prayer is a powerful weapon in tearing down strongholds. Through fervent prayer and intercession, we can petition God to intervene in our lives and break the chains of bondage. We can pray for God's strength, wisdom, and guidance as we confront the enemy and his strongholds.

5. Standing on God's Promises:

As we engage in spiritual warfare, we must stand firmly on the promises of God's Word. Scriptures such as 2 Corinthians 10:4-5 remind us that the weapons of our warfare are not carnal but mighty in God for pulling down strongholds. By declaring God's promises and truths over our lives, we declare victory over the enemy.

6. Community and Accountability:

Breaking strongholds is often a challenging journey that requires support and accountability. Surrounding ourselves with fellow believers who can pray for us, encourage us, and hold us accountable is essential. Together, we can stand united against the enemy and overcome the strongholds in our lives.

7. Persistence and Perseverance:

Breaking strongholds may not happen overnight; it requires persistence and perseverance. We must be willing to press on in faith, even when the battle seems fierce. By continually seeking God, resisting the enemy, and standing firm in our identity in Christ, we will experience victory over the strongholds that once held us captive.

In conclusion, breaking strongholds in deliverance ministry is a spiritual battle that requires diligence, faith, and reliance on God's power. By identifying strongholds, engaging in spiritual warfare, and standing on God's promises, we can experience freedom and transformation in Christ. As we renounce sin, repent of wrongdoing, and rely on the Holy Spirit, we will see strongholds torn down and lives restored to wholeness in Him.

Example Prayer:

Heavenly Father,

I come before you recognizing the stronghold of [name the specific stronghold, e.g., addiction, fear, unforgiveness] in my life. I acknowledge that this stronghold has held me captive for too long, hindering my relationship with you and others. I renounce any agreement I have made with the enemy and repent of any sin that has allowed this stronghold to take root in my life.

In the name of Jesus, I command this stronghold to be broken and dismantled. I declare that I am no longer a slave to fear, addiction, or any other form of bondage. By the power of your Holy Spirit, I tear down every wall the enemy has erected in my mind, heart, and spirit.

Lord, I ask you to fill me afresh with your presence and strength. Help me to stand firm on your promises and to resist the schemes of the enemy. Surround me with your angels of protection and warfare as I engage in spiritual battle.

I declare that I am more than a conqueror through Christ who strengthens me. I refuse to be defined by my past or by the lies of the enemy. I am a child of God, redeemed by the blood of Jesus, and nothing can separate me from your love.

Thank you, Lord, for the victory that is mine in Christ Jesus. I receive your freedom, your peace, and your joy as I walk in obedience to your Word. May your kingdom come and your will be done in my life, as it is in heaven.

In Jesus' mighty name, I pray. Amen.

CHAPTER 29:
The Importance of Inner Healing in Deliverance Ministry

In the journey of deliverance ministry, we find that inner healing plays a pivotal role in addressing the emotional and spiritual wounds that can open doors to demonic oppression. Let us explore the significance of inner healing in light of the Scriptures.

1. Addressing Root Causes:

- Psalm 147:3 (NIV): "He heals the brokenhearted and binds up their wounds."
- Isaiah 61:1 (NIV):"The Spirit of the Sovereign Lord is on me, because the Lord has anointed me to proclaim good news to the poor. He has sent me to bind up the brokenhearted, to proclaim freedom for the captives and release from darkness for the prisoners."

2. Breaking Generational Patterns:

- Exodus 20:5-6 (NIV): "You shall not bow down to them or worship them; for I, the Lord your God, am a jealous God, punishing the children for the sin of the parents to the third and fourth generation of those who hate me, but showing love to a thousand generations of those who love me and keep my commandments."
- Galatians 3:13-14 (NIV): "Christ redeemed us from the curse of the law by becoming a curse for us, for it is written: 'Cursed is everyone who is hung on a pole.' He redeemed us in order that the blessing given to Abraham might come to the Gentiles through Christ Jesus, so that by faith we might receive the promise of the Spirit."

3. Restoring Identity and Worth:

- 2 Corinthians 5:17 (NIV): "Therefore, if anyone is in Christ, the new creation has come: The old has gone, the new is here!"
- Ephesians 1:4-5 (NIV): "For he chose us in him before the creation of the world to be holy and blameless in his sight. In love he predestined us for adoption to sonship through Jesus Christ, in accordance with his pleasure and will—"

4. Releasing Forgiveness and Reconciliation:

- Colossians 3:13 (NIV): "Bear with each other and forgive one another if any of you has a grievance against someone. Forgive as the Lord forgave you."

- Matthew 6:14-15 (NIV): "For if you forgive other people when they sin against you, your heavenly Father will also forgive you. But if you do not forgive others their sins, your Father will not forgive your sins."

5. Cultivating Wholeness and Holiness:

- 1 Thessalonians 5:23 (NIV): "May God himself, the God of peace, sanctify you through and through. May your whole spirit, soul and body be kept blameless at the coming of our Lord Jesus Christ."
- Romans 12:2 (NIV): "Do not conform to the pattern of this world, but be transformed by the renewing of your mind. Then you will be able to test and approve what God's will is—his good, pleasing and perfect will."

Conclusion:

Incorporating inner healing into deliverance ministry aligns with God's desire for His people to experience wholeness, freedom, and restoration in every area of their lives. By addressing emotional wounds, breaking generational curses, restoring identity, releasing forgiveness, and cultivating holiness, individuals can walk in the fullness of God's purposes and promises. As ministers of deliverance, let us continue to seek the guidance of the Holy Spirit in facilitating inner healing for those in need, knowing that it is through His power and grace that true transformation occurs.

Example Inner Healing Prayer:

Heavenly Father, I come before you with a humble and contrite heart, recognizing the wounds and hurts that have burdened me for so long. I acknowledge that only You, Lord, have the power to bring healing and restoration to my soul.

I bring before You now all the pain, trauma, and brokenness I have experienced throughout my life. I ask for Your healing touch to come upon every area of my heart and mind that has been affected by these wounds.

Lord Jesus, I invite You into the deepest recesses of my being, where the scars of past hurts reside. Pour out Your healing balm upon me, washing away every tear, every fear, and every ounce of pain. Replace them with Your peace that surpasses all understanding.

Father, I lift up to You every memory that has caused me anguish and torment. I ask that You would heal the wounds of these memories and replace them with Your truth and love. Help me to see myself and others through Your eyes, as cherished and valued children of God.

I renounce any bitterness, unforgiveness, or resentment that I have been holding onto. I release it all into Your hands, knowing that You are the ultimate healer and restorer. Give me the strength and grace to forgive those who have wronged me, just as You have forgiven me.

Lord, I ask for Your wisdom and discernment to identify any generational curses or patterns of sin that have been passed down through my family line. By Your power, break every chain that binds me to these curses, and set me free to walk in the fullness of Your blessings.

Holy Spirit, come and minister to the deepest parts of my soul, bringing wholeness and healing to every broken area. Fill me afresh with Your love, joy, and peace, and empower me to live victoriously in Christ.

Thank You, Lord, for Your faithfulness and unfailing love. I receive Your healing touch with gratitude and trust, knowing that You are making all things new in my life. In Jesus' name, I pray. Amen.

CHAPTER 30:

Deliverance
Ministry Model

In the realm of deliverance ministry, a structured approach to exorcism is essential for effectively confronting demonic forces and facilitating spiritual freedom. Here, we outline a comprehensive model comprising five key components to guide practitioners through the process of spiritual warfare and deliverance.

1. Intake Questions

a. Assessment: Commence by thoroughly reviewing intake questions with the client to discern any indicators of demonic influence. Look for patterns of behavior, experiences, or spiritual encounters that may suggest demonic oppression or possession. Compile a detailed renouncement and repentance list based on the information gathered.

b. Identification: During this phase, identify any ungodly soul ties that may contribute to the client's spiritual bondage. These ties must be recognized and severed to facilitate freedom and healing.

2. Renouncement/Repentance

a. Prayer: Lead the client in prayers of renouncement, repentance, and forgiveness as needed. Guide them through acknowledging and rejecting any agreements or affiliations with the enemy.

b. Preparation: Ensure completion of the renouncement process before permitting any demonic manifestations. Establish a foundation of repentance and spiritual cleansing before engaging in direct confrontation with demonic forces.

c. Soul Tie Breaking: Address any ungodly soul ties identified during intake. Lead the client in breaking these ties, severing any unhealthy connections hindering their spiritual freedom.

d. Inner Healing: Explore opportunities for inner healing as part of the renouncement process. Encourage the client to confront and address past wounds, traumas, or unresolved issues contributing to their spiritual oppression.

3. Interrogation of Demons

a. Engagement: Seek the manifestation of demons, actively probing for their presence and influence in the client's life. Encourage openness and transparency as you confront these forces of darkness.

b. Identification: Identify the chief demon and subordinate demons under its authority. Document their names and roles within the spiritual hierarchy to gain insight into specific manifestations of evil.

4. Generational Curse Breaking

a. Examination: Interrogate the chief demon to uncover any generational curses affecting the client's bloodline. Investigate both paternal and maternal lineages to understand the origins and implications of these curses.

b. Intervention: Guide the client in breaking generational curses through prayer and spiritual warfare. Lead them in renouncing and rejecting these curses, releasing themselves and future generations from their bondage.

5. Expulsion

a. Binding: Instruct the chief demon to bind all subordinate demons, consolidating their authority under its command to ensure a unified approach to expulsion.

b. Liberation: Direct the chief demon to lift the generational curse from the client and future generations, releasing them from its oppressive influence. Command the demon to relinquish anything held in bondage by the curse.

c. Judgment: Bind the chief demon to God's judgment, affirming its defeat and expulsion from the client's life.

d. Expulsion Protocol: Lead the chief demon through the expulsion protocol, commanding it to depart from the client's mind and body using the authority of Jesus Christ.

In summary, this exorcism model provides a structured framework for conducting deliverance ministry with precision and effectiveness. By following these five components, practitioners can navigate spiritual warfare and lead individuals to freedom and wholeness in Christ.

CHAPTER 31:
Conclusion
and Summary

Throughout this comprehensive guide to deliverance ministry, we've embarked on a profound journey into the realm of spiritual warfare, exploring the intricacies of demonic oppression and the pathways to freedom found in Christ. Each chapter has served as a beacon of illumination, shedding light on crucial principles, practices, and prayers that empower both practitioners and individuals seeking deliverance to navigate the complexities of spiritual battles and emerge victorious.

In our exploration, we've underscored the critical significance of:

1. Spiritual Discernment: Cultivating a keen awareness of the signs of demonic influence and developing a deep understanding of the spiritual landscapes we encounter. (Hebrews 5:14)

2. Prayer and Intercession: Engaging in fervent, earnest prayer and intercession to beseech God's divine intervention and sovereign authority in the deliverance process. (Philippians 4:6-7)

3. Repentance and Renunciation: Embracing a posture of humility and contrition, acknowledging and renouncing all ungodly ties, and wholeheartedly turning to God in genuine repentance as the foundational steps toward liberation. (James 4:7-8)

4. Scriptural Foundation: Anchoring our beliefs and practices firmly in the unshakeable truths of God's Word, which serves as our ultimate weapon and source of authority against the forces of darkness. (2 Timothy 3:16-17)

5. Authority in Christ: Embracing and wielding the authority bestowed upon us as heirs of Christ, understanding that through Him, we possess the power to confront and conquer the principalities and powers of darkness. (Luke 10:19)

6. Holistic Healing: Recognizing the holistic nature of deliverance ministry, which encompasses spiritual, emotional, and physical healing, including inner healing and the breaking of generational curses. (Psalm 147:3)

7. Persistence and Perseverance: Upholding unwavering faith and steadfast perseverance in the face of spiritual opposition, trusting in the unfailing faithfulness of God to bring about triumphant victory. (Hebrews 10:35-36)

As we draw this journey to a close, let us carry forward the profound truths and transformative insights gleaned from our exploration of deliverance ministry. May we continue to walk boldly in the light of Christ's truth, armed with the knowledge, authority, and compassion He has bestowed upon us. And may His name be exalted and glorified in every victory won and every life transformed through the ministry of deliverance. Amen.

Heavenly Father,

We come before Your throne with hearts filled with reverence and awe, acknowledging Your sovereignty over all creation. You are the Alpha and the Omega, the beginning and the end, the Almighty God who reigns forevermore. We humbly bow before You, recognizing Your supreme authority in every realm, including the spiritual battles we face.

Lord Jesus Christ, we exalt Your holy name above all names. You are the King of Kings and the Lord of Lords, the Commander of angelic hosts and the Conqueror of darkness. It is in Your mighty name that we engage in spiritual warfare, for You have given us authority to trample on serpents and scorpions and to overcome all the power of the enemy.

We honor You, Jesus, as the Victor over sin and death, the Lamb who was slain for our redemption. By Your precious blood shed on Calvary's cross, You have purchased our freedom from bondage and delivered us from the domain of darkness into Your marvelous light. We declare that there is no power or principality that can stand against You, for You have triumphed over them all.

As we engage in spiritual warfare, we place our trust in Your unfailing strength and unfathomable love. Empower us with Your Holy Spirit to wield the sword of the Spirit, which is the Word of God, with precision and effectiveness. Grant us discernment to recognize the schemes of the enemy and wisdom to navigate every spiritual battle with courage and faith.

May every victory won in spiritual warfare be a testimony to Your mighty power and unfailing grace. Let Your name be glorified as chains are broken, captives are set free, and lives are transformed by Your saving grace. We surrender ourselves afresh to Your will, knowing that in You, we have the victory.

In Jesus' name, we pray,
Amen.

SPIRITUAL WARFARE :
ARMING THE SAINTS
BOOK 1

Pastor Miguel Bustillos

Made in United States
Troutdale, OR
08/21/2024

22208913R00076